FINANCIAL INSTITUTIONS AND SERVICES

THE OVERSEAS PRIVATE INVESTMENT CORPORATION

DEVELOPMENT ASSISTANCE OVERVIEW, PROJECT SELECTION AND MONITORING PRACTICES

FINANCIAL INSTITUTIONS AND SERVICES

Additional books in this series can be found on Nova's website under the Series tab.

Additional e-books in this series can be found on Nova's website under the e-book tab.

FINANCIAL INSTITUTIONS AND SERVICES

THE OVERSEAS PRIVATE INVESTMENT CORPORATION

DEVELOPMENT ASSISTANCE OVERVIEW, PROJECT SELECTION AND MONITORING PRACTICES

MOLLY H. WALSH
EDITOR

NOVINKA

New York

NOTICE TO THE READER

Library of Congress Cataloging-in-Publication Data

ISBN: 978-1-63485-728-4

Published by Nova Science Publishers, Inc. † New York

CONTENTS

PREFACE

The Overseas Private Investment Corporation (OPIC), a wholly-owned U.S. government corporation, is referred to as the U.S. development finance institution (DFI). It provides political risk insurance, project and investment funds financing, and other services to promote U.S. direct investment in developing countries and emerging economies that will have a development impact. It operates under the foreign policy guidance of the Secretary of State. OPIC's governing legislation is the Foreign Assistance Act of 1961, as amended. This book discusses OPIC background; international context for development finance; and key issues for Congress related to OPIC. Furthermore, the book assesses OPIC's monitoring processes to ensure risks associated with current practices are acceptable for meeting OPIC's program goals.

In: The Overseas Private Investment Corporation ISBN: 978-1-63485-728-4
Editor: Molly H. Walsh

Chapter 1

THE OVERSEAS PRIVATE INVESTMENT CORPORATION: BACKGROUND AND LEGISLATIVE ISSUES*

Shayerah Ilias Akhtar

SUMMARY

The Overseas Private Investment Corporation (OPIC), a wholly-owned U.S. government corporation, is referred to as the U.S. development finance institution (DFI). It provides political risk insurance, project and investment funds financing, and other services to promote U.S. direct investment in developing countries and emerging economies that will have a development impact. It operates under the foreign policy guidance of the Secretary of State. OPIC's governing legislation is the Foreign Assistance Act of 1961, as amended (22 U.S.C. §2191 *et seq.*).

Congress periodically has extended OPIC's authority to conduct its programs. The most recent multi-year, stand-alone reauthorization took place in 2003 with legislation extending its authority until September 30, 2007 (P.L. 108-158). Over the past several years, Congress has extended OPIC's authority through the appropriations process. The FY2015 appropriations act (§7073(b) of P.L. 113-235) extends OPIC's authority to conduct its credit and insurance programs until September 30, 2015. In

* This is an edited, reformatted and augmented version of a Congressional Research Service, Publication No. 98-567, dated August 20, 2015.

addition to authorization responsibilities, Congress has appropriations, oversight, and other legislative responsibilities related to OPIC.

OPIC's programs are intended to promote U.S. private investment in developing countries by mitigating risks, such as political risks (including currency inconvertibility, expropriation, and political violence). Its financing and insurance are backed by the full faith and credit of the U.S. government. Congress places statutory requirements on OPIC's activities, such as those related to the economic and environmental impacts of projects. In FY2014, OPIC support was available in over 160 countries around the world and across a range of economic sectors. According to OPIC, since it began operations, it has supported more than 4,300 investment projects of more than $225 billion in investment value.

The international context in which OPIC operates has evolved. Foreign direct investment (FDI) flows have overtaken official development assistance (ODA) flows as a primary source of external financing to developing countries. DFIs also are playing a more active role in supporting private sector capital flows to developing countries. The composition of DFI players, historically dominated by developed countries, also has evolved, with emerging markets such as China becoming more prominent. Presently, OPIC has many counterparts at the bilateral, regional, and multilateral levels.

OPIC states that it operates on a "self-sustaining basis," using its own revenues, which include user fees and interest from U.S. Treasury securities. However, Congress annually sets in legislation OPIC's maximum spending levels for its administrative and program expenses. For FY2015, Congress provided $62.8 million for OPIC's administrative expenses to carry out its credit and insurance programs and authorized a transfer of $25.0 million from OPIC's noncredit account for credit program costs.

The 114th Congress may take up a number of issues related to OPIC. A key issue is whether or not to renew OPIC's authority and, if so, under what terms. Perspectives on OPIC differ. Supporters highlight OPIC's role in filling gaps in private sector investment financing and political risk insurance and helping to level the playing field for U.S. businesses vis-à-vis foreign competitors. Critics argue that OPIC is a form of "corporate welfare," with the private sector better suited to conduct such services, and they question OPIC's development benefits. Congress also may examine OPIC's financial product offerings, policies, activity composition, and organizational structure.

The Overseas Private Investment Corporation (OPIC) is a wholly-owned U.S. government corporation that seeks to promote economic growth in less developed economies through the mobilization of private capital, in support of

U.S. foreign policy goals.[1] It is often referred to as the U.S. government's development finance institution (DFI).[2]

OPIC's enabling legislation is the Foreign Assistance Act of 1961 (P.L. 87-195), as amended.[3] The Foreign Assistance Act provides OPIC with authority to conduct its activities for a renewable period of time.[4] The latest multi-year, standalone reauthorization of OPIC was in legislation passed in 2003 (P.L. 108-158) that extended OPIC's authority until September 30, 2007. Over the past several years, Congress has renewed OPIC's authority through the appropriations process (i.e., essentially through a "reauthorization waiver"). Most recently, the FY2015 appropriations act (§7073(b) of P.L. 113-235) extends OPIC's authority to conduct its credit and insurance programs until September 30, 2015.[5]

The Foreign Assistance Act directs OPIC to, "mobilize and facilitate the participation of United States private capital and skills in the economic and social development of less developed countries and areas, and countries in transition from nonmarket to market economies ... under the policy guidance of the Secretary of State."[6] OPIC works to fulfill its mandate by providing political risk insurance, project and investment funds financing, and other services to promote U.S. direct investment oveseas. Its services are intended to mitigate the risks affecting U.S. international investment, such as political risks (including currency inconvertibility, expropriation, and political violence), for U.S. firms making qualified investments overseas.[7] OPIC characterizes itself as "demand-driven," providing services based on user interest. OPIC's activities may support U.S. exports, and it is involved in U.S. trade promotion interagency processes and initiatives.[8]

Congress does not approve individual OPIC projects, but has authorization, appropriations, oversight, and other legislative responsibilities related to the agency and its activities. Congress authorizes OPIC's ability to conduct its credit and insurance programs for a period of time that it chooses; can amend or change its governing legislation as it deems appropriate; and approves an annual appropriation for OPIC that sets an upper limit on the agency's administrative and program expenses, which are covered by OPIC's own funds. The Senate confirms presidential appointments to OPIC's Board of Directors and to the OPIC positions of president and executive vice president. The 114th Congress may take up a number of issues related to OPIC, chief of which could be whether to renew OPIC's authority and, if so, under what terms. Congress also may examine OPIC's financial product offerings, policies, activity composition, and organizational structure.

This report is structured into three parts: (1) OPIC background; (2) international context for development finance; and (3) key issues for Congress related to OPIC.

BACKGROUND

Origins

Created under the Foreign Assistance Act of 1961 (P.L. 87-195) as amended, OPIC was established in 1969 and began operations in 1971 as a development finance institution amid an atmosphere of congressional disillusionment overall with U.S. aid programs, especially large infrastructure projects. In his first message to Congress on aid, President Nixon recommended the creation of OPIC to assume the investment guaranty and promotion functions that were being conducted by the U.S. Agency for International Development (USAID). President Nixon also directed that OPIC would provide "businesslike management of investment incentives" to contribute to the economic and social progress of developing nations.[9]

In creating OPIC, the Nixon Administration indicated that it was not attempting to end official U.S. foreign assistance, because "private capital and technical assistance cannot substitute for government assistance programs," a combination that can provide "official aid on the one hand, and private investment and technical assistance on the other." Private investment activities, however, were meant to complement the official assistance programs and, thereby, multiply the benefits of both. In addition, market-oriented private investment was viewed as an antidote to the government-oriented aid projects that were considered by some to be costly and inefficient. OPIC was created as a first step in the eventual overhaul of the entire U.S. aid program. In 1973, this overhaul was completed as the United States largely abandoned infrastructure building and other large capital projects in favor of humanitarian aid to meet basic human needs.[10]

Programs

OPIC categorizes its operations into three main programs—insurance, finance, and investment funds—that are intended to promote U.S. private investment in less developed countries by mitigating risks, such as political risks, for U.S. firms making qualified investment overseas. OPIC's authority to guarantee and insure U.S. investments abroad is backed by the full faith and credit of the U.S. government and OPIC's own financial resources. OPIC provides financing and insurance coverage of up to $250 million per project.

While private sector markets exist for financing and insuring U.S. direct investment overseas, there may be gaps in them due to "market failures" such as imperfect information, barriers to entry, risk levels, and financial crises. OPIC's primary objective in operating its programs is to promote economic development in low-income countries by supporting investment in projects, economic sectors, regions, and countries that are underserved by private markets; and mobilizing private investment in countries with viable project environments, but low credit ratings. For example, individual firms may attach more risk to investing in developing economies due to imperfect information and, thus, be unwilling to commit resources to investments in the least developed countries without risk mitigation by OPIC through its financing and insurance support.[11]

Political Risk Insurance

OPIC provides political risk insurance to safeguard investments against certain political risks involved in investing in developing countries in three broad areas:

- **Currency inconvertibility** coverage compensates investors if new currency restrictions are imposed which prevent the conversion and transfer of remittances from insured investments, but does not protect against currency devaluation.
- **Expropriation** coverage protects U.S. firms against the nationalization, confiscation, or expropriation of an enterprise, including actions by foreign governments that deprive an investor of fundamental rights or financial interests in a project for a period of at least six months. This coverage excludes losses that may arise from lawful regulatory or revenue actions by a foreign government and actions instigated or provoked by the investor or foreign firm.
- **Political violence** coverage compensates U.S. citizens and firms for property and income losses directly caused by various kinds of violence, including declared or undeclared wars, hostile actions by national or international forces, civil war, revolution, insurrection, and civil strife (including politically motivated terrorism and sabotage). Income loss insurance protects the investor's share of income from

> losses that result from damage to the insured property caused by political violence. Assets coverage compensates U.S. citizens and firms for losses of or damage to tangible property caused by political violence. OPIC also has a number of special programs that protect U.S. banks from political violence. This type of insurance reduces risks for banks and other institutional investors, which allows them to play a more active role in financing projects in developing countries. Specialized types of insurance coverage also are available for U.S. investors involved with certain contracting, exporting, licensing, or leasing transactions that are undertaken in a developing country.

OPIC's political risk insurance is available to U.S. citizens, U.S. firms, or to the foreign subsidiaries of U.S. firms as long as the foreign subsidiary is at least 95% owned by a U.S. citizen. According to OPIC, such insurance is available for investments in new ventures or in expansions of existing enterprises, and can cover equity investments, parent company and third party loans and loan guarantees, technical assistance agreements, cross-border leases, assigned inventory or equipment, and other forms of investment.[12]

Investment Financing

OPIC's investment financing program operates like an investment bank, customizing and structuring a complete package for individual projects in countries where conventional financing institutions often are unwilling or unable to lend on a basis that is competitively advantageous for investors. Most OPIC financing for a "non-financial" industry project (e.g., energy, manufacturing, transportation) is used to cover capital costs, such as facility construction or leasehold improvements, equipment, and design and engineering services associated with establishing or expanding a project. For a financial industry project, OPIC financing is used to fund lending capacity expansion, such as for microfinance, small- and medium-sized enterprise (SME) lending, or mortgage lending, by a financial services provider.[13]

To obtain OPIC financing, the venture must be commercially and financially sound and have some portion of U.S. ownership. Projects may be wholly owned by U.S. companies, foreign subsidiaries of U.S. companies, or joint ventures involving local companies and U.S. sponsored firms. In the case of a joint venture involving existing firms, the U.S. investor generally is expected to own at least 25% of the equity of the project. For new ventures, financing may be equal to 50% of the total project cost; a larger share is possible for certain projects.

The amount of OPIC's participation may vary taking into consideration financial risks and benefits. In general, OPIC will not support more than 75% of the total investment. OPIC provides financing to investors through two major programs: direct loans and loan guarantees.

- **Direct loans** generally range between $350,000 and $50 million, but can be more in certain cases. Direct loans are available only for ventures sponsored by, or significantly involving, U.S. SMEs or cooperatives (e.g., joint ventures).
- **Loan guarantees** typically are used for larger projects, ranging in size up to $250 million, but in certain cases can be higher. OPIC's guarantees are issued to financial institutions that are more than 50% owned by U.S. citizens, corporations, or partnerships. Rates and conditions on loans and guarantees depend on financial market conditions at the time and on OPIC's assessment of the financial and political risks involved. Consistent with commercial lending practices, OPIC charges up-front, commitment, and cancellation fees, and reimbursement is required for project-related expenses.

As part of its emphasis on U.S. small business investors, OPIC established the Enterprise Development Network (EDN) in June 2007. Under the EDN, OPIC collaborates with participating financial intermediaries to expand access of small businesses to OPIC-supported products and services.[14]

Investment Funds

Investment funds are privately owned and managed sources of capital that make direct equity investments in portfolio companies in new, expanding or privatizing companies in developing or emerging markets. OPIC supports these funds through financing to supplement the equity that the funds privately raise. In most instances, OPIC provides up to one-third of the fund's total capital, and receives debt returns on its investment. OPIC takes a senior creditor position.

OPIC supports these funds in situations where U.S. firms either cannot allocate or cannot raise sufficient capital to start or expand their businesses overseas. OPIC solicits these funds through a competitive "Call for Proposals" process that seeks investment funds focusing on the agency's development priorities, particularly in areas where investments have been difficult to obtain. OPIC uses the "Call for Proposals" process to select fund managers with private equity investment capability and experience. OPIC-supported investment funds cover a range of economic sectors, including financial services, insurance, housing, renewable energy, and information technology.[15]

OPIC approved its first investment fund in 1987.[16] The investment funds program has been restructured periodically, such as in 2002, leading to the incorporation of the competitive selection process through the "Call for Proposals" (discussed above).[17]

Other Activities

OPIC conducts outreach to raise awareness of its programs and services for U.S. investors. For instance, OPIC offers workshops and seminars as part of its *Expanding Horizons* program to address concerns over political risks in emerging markets and share information about its programs and resources to support overseas investment. *Expanding Horizons* includes a focus on supporting U.S. small businesses in expanding to overseas markets.[18]

Statutory and Policy Conditions for OPIC-Supported Projects

Congress does not approve individual OPIC projects, but sets forth specific statutory requirements for OPIC in the Foreign Assistance Act of 1961 (22 U.S.C. §2191 *et seq.*), as amended. OPIC also has various policy requirements for its support (see Table 1).

OPIC investment support falls outside of the international rules of the OECD Arrangement on Officially Supported Export Credits (the Arrangement)—which establishes guidelines for member countries' export credit agencies (ECAs), such as the Export-Import Bank of the United States (Ex-Im Bank).[19] The Arrangement establishes limitations on terms and conditions of ECAs, including on minimum interest rates, maximum repayment terms, notification procedures, and reporting requirements for government-supported export credit activity that is directly tied to exports.[20] Among other things, the Arrangement does *not* apply to investment support not directly linked or tied to procurement from the United States.[21] As such, OPIC's activities are considered to fall outside of the OECD Arrangement (though they nevertheless may contribute to U.S. exports).

Table 1. Overview of Selected Statutory and Policy Requirements for OPIC

Requirement	Description	Statutory Basis
OVERALL		
Mandate	OPIC's mandate is "[t]o mobilize and facilitate the participation of United States private capital and skills in the economic and social development of less developed countries and areas, and countries in transition from nonmarket to market economies, thereby complementing the development assistance objectives of the United States... under the foreign policy guidance of the Secretary of State."	22 U.S.C. §2191
Repayment	OPIC is directed to operate "on a self-sustaining basis, taking into account in its financing operations the economic and financial soundness of projects[.]"	22 U.S.C. §2191(a)
TRANSACTION-SPECIFIC		
U.S. Connection	According to OPIC, projects that it supports must have "meaningful involvement" by a U.S. citizen or business. OPIC's enabling legislation defines the term "eligible investor," and its policies provide further specifications.	22 U.S.C. §2198(c)
Economic Impact	In determining whether to provide support, OPIC shall "be guided by the economic and social impact and benefits" of the project, and seek to support "those developmental projects having positive trade benefits for the United States[.]" OPIC must decline support if it determines that overseas investment may reduce employment in United States, either because the U.S. firm shifts part of its production abroad, or because output from overseas investment will be shipped to United States and "reduce substantially the positive trade benefits" of the investment.	22 U.S.C. §2191(1); 22 U.S.C. §2191(i),(k)-(m)
Environmental Impact	OPIC generally is barred from participating in projects that pose an "unreasonable or major environmental health, or safety, hazard...."	22 U.S.C. §2191(n); 22 U.S. §2191a(b)

Table 1. (Continued)

Requirement	Description	Statutory Basis
	The Board of Directors cannot vote in favor of any project likely to have "significant adverse environmental impacts that are sensitive, diverse, or unprecedented" unless at least 60 days before the date of the vote, an environmental impact assessment of the project is conducted and made publicly available.	
Worker Rights	Projects can be implemented only in countries that currently have, or are taking steps to adopt and implement, laws that uphold internationally recognized worker rights. A national economic interest determination waiver is possible by the President of the United States.	22 U.S.C. §2191a(a)
Human Rights	OPIC is required to take into account in conducting its programs in a country, in consultation with the Secretary of State, "all available information about observance of and respect for human rights and fundamental freedoms in such country and the effect the operation of such programs will have on human rights and fundamental freedoms in such country."	22 U.S.C. §2199(i)
Small Business	To the "maximum degree possible consistent with its purposes," OPIC must give preferential consideration to projects involving U.S. small business and to increase the proportion of projects significantly involving U.S. small business to at least 30% of certain of its activity.	22 U.S.C. §2191(e)
Additionality	It is OPIC policy that its activities should complement, rather than compete with, the private sector, i.e., transactions that would otherwise be impossible or unlikely without its support.	
FOCUS AREAS AND LIMITATIONS		
Renewable Energy	FY2010 appropriations language directed OPIC to "issue a report, not later than 180 days after December 16, 2009, highlighting its substantial commitment to invest in renewable and other clean energy technologies and plans to	P.L. 111-117, 7079(b);22 U.S.C. §2191b

Requirement	Description	Statutory Basis
	significantly reduce greenhouse gas emissions from its portfolio," with the proviso that "such commitment shall include implementing a revised climate change mitigation plan to reduce greenhouse gas emissions associated with projects and sub-projects in the agency's portfolio as of June 30, 2008 by at least 30 percent over a 10-year period and by at least 50 percent over a 15-year period."	
Coal-fired Power Plants	Under FY2015 appropriations legislation, the use of OPIC funds is prohibited, through September 30, 2015, under certain conditions, for the enforcement of any rule, regulation, policy, or guidelines implemented pursuant to: • OPIC's greenhouse gas emissions reductions policy, based on FY2010 appropriations language (see above); and • OPIC's proposed modification to its Environmental and Social Policy Statement (ESPS) related to coal.	P.L. 113-235, 7086(4)(A)-(B))
Sub-Saharan Africa	The Board of Directors is directed to take "prompt measures" to increase OPIC programs and financial commitments in sub-Saharan Africa.	22 U.S.C. §2193(e)
Country Restrictions	"From time to time, statutory and policy constraints may limit the availability of OPIC programs in certain countries, or countries where programs were previously unavailable may become eligible."	
Sectoral and Product Restrictions	OPIC has "categorically prohibited sectors" based on economic, environmental, and other policy, e.g., projects established as a result of reducing or terminating U.S.-based operations.	

Source: CRS analysis of OPIC's enabling legislation (22 U.S.C. §2191 *et seq.*), as well as OPIC website and publications.

Notes: Descriptions provide summaries of the requirements and may not be comprehensive.

Portfolio Exposure

The statutory limit on the total contingent liability ("portfolio exposure") for OPIC's financing and insurance is $29 billion.[22] In FY2014, OPIC's portfolio had a total exposure of $18 billion distributed across financial products and regions (see Figure 1 and Table 2).[23]

The composition of OPIC's portfolio by financial product type has evolved; in earlier years, political risk insurance constituted the larger share of the portfolio, while in more recent years, investment financing constitutes the larger share. For example, in FY2000, OPIC's total portfolio of $16.8 billion was composed of 59% in political risk insurance and 41% in investment financing.[24] In contrast, in FY2014, OPIC's total portfolio of $18 billion was composed of 17% in political risk insurance and 83% in investment financing.[25]

Table 2. Composition of OPIC Portfolio Exposure, FY2014

Exposure Category	Amount ($bn)	Percent of Total Exposurc
Total Exposure	$18.0	100%
Program		
Financing (Loan, Loan Guarantee, Funds Support)	$15.0	83%
Political Risk Insurance	$3.1	17%
Geographic Region		
Latin American and the Caribbean	$5.5	30%
Sub-Saharan Africa	$3.7	20%
North Africa/Middle East	$3.3	18%
Eastern Europe and Newly Industrializing States	$3.0	17%
Asia	$2.6	14%
Worldwide Funds	$0.7	4%
Stop Loss Adjustments[a]	-$0.6	-4%

Source: CRS, based on data from Annual Management Report of the Overseas Private Investment Corporation for Fiscal Year 2014, p. 9.

Notes: The OPIC publication did not provide exposure composition by economic sector.

[a] According to OPIC's FY2013 annual management report, the insurance stop-loss adjustment "represents the difference between the aggregate coverage amount and OPIC's actual exposure under these contracts."

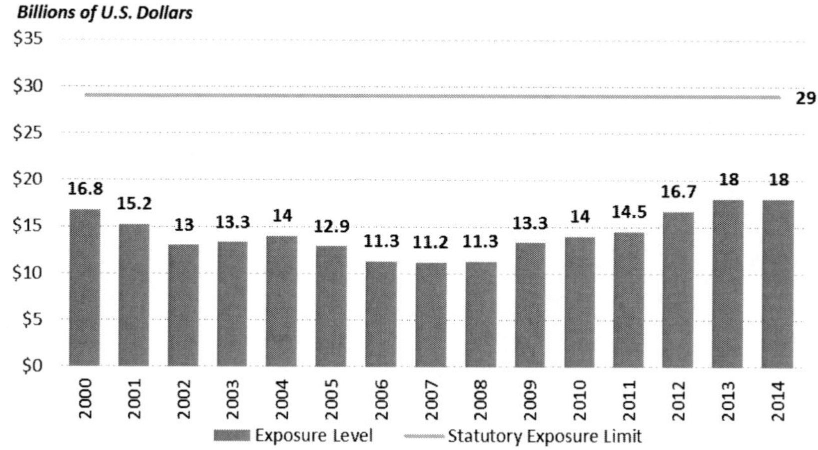

Source: CRS, based on data from OPIC annual reports, various years.
Notes: OPIC's statutory limit on its exposure is provided in 22 U.S.C. §2195(a).

Figure 1. OPIC Portfolio Exposure: Statutory Limit and Actual Level, FY2000-2014.

Authorizations of Finance and Insurance Support

In FY2014, OPIC provided $2.96 billion in new commitments for investment projects (see **Figure 2**), which it estimates will support $316 million in U.S. exports over the next five years.[26] It also estimates that its FY2014 new commitments are associated with 409 jobs in the United States and 9,000 jobs in the host countries.[27] OPIC prioritizes its works based on U.S. foreign policy and development objectives, but is also demand-driven. Activities include the following.[28]

- **Countries/regions:** In FY2014, OPIC support was available in 162 developing and emerging economies across Africa, Latin America, the Middle East, Asia, and Eastern Europe.[29] OPIC had active projects in 101 countries that year. According to OPIC, 31% of the new projects to which it committed support in FY2014 were in poor countries.[30] OPIC's support for projects in sub-Saharan Africa has grown from around 6% about a decade ago to around one-quarter of new commitments in FY2014.[31]
- **Economics sectors:** OPIC is active in a range of economic sectors, including agriculture, renewable energy, health care, financial

services, housing, infrastructure, "impact investing," and technology.[32] Between FY2010 and FY2014, its renewable energy commitments nearly doubled to $1.22 billion.[33] OPIC considers all of its projects to be in "impact sectors," but specified that its FY2014 activity included $188 million for projects "with the explicit intention of promoting social and environmental returns in addition to financial returns."[34]

- **SMEs:** OPIC seeks to expand U.S. SME involvement in overseas investment. According to OPIC, between FY2010 and FY2014, U.S. SMEs accounted for nearly 75% of projects receiving its support.[35] OPIC also has focused on expanding financing available to SMEs in developing countries and emerging markets.

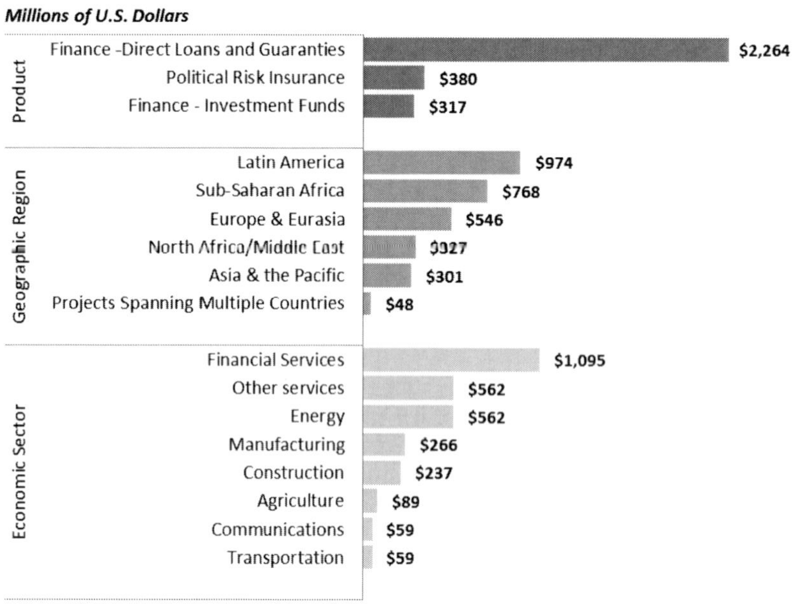

Source: CRS, based on *OPIC 2014 Annual Report*; and U.S. Congress, House Committee on Foreign Affairs, Subcommittee on Terrorism, Nonproliferation, and Trade, *Testimony by Elizabeth Littlefield, President and CEO, OPIC*, Hearing on "Trade Promotion Agencies and U.S. Foreign Policy," 114th Cong., 1st sess., May 19, 2015.

Notes: OPIC FY2014 new commitments totaled $2.96 billion. The economic sector values reflect CRS calculations using the worldwide commitment and percentages for each economic sector from the testimony.

Figure 2. Composition of OPIC New Commitments, FY2014.

OPIC participates in broader foreign policy initiatives by the Administration, as illustrated below.

- In **response to political change in the MENA region**, in March 2011, then-Secretary of State Clinton announced that OPIC would provide up to $2 billion in financial support "to catalyze private sector development" in MENA to spur economic growth and job creation.[36] In May 2011, President Obama announced that OPIC would provide up to $1 billion in financing to support infrastructure and job creation specifically in Egypt.[37] As part of these efforts, OPIC, for example, approved $500 million in lending to Egypt and Jordan ($250 million to each country) to support small businesses in those countries.[38]
- The **U.S.-Africa Clean Energy Finance (ACEF) Initiative**—a joint mechanism by OPIC, along with the Department of State and the Trade and Development Agency (TDA)—is a four-year, $20 million program launched in June 2012 to catalyze private sector investment in the African clean energy sector by identifying and providing financing for project development costs. In 2013, OPIC dedicated a staff member for South Africa to support the initiative.[39]
- The **U.S.-Asia Pacific Comprehensive Partnership for a Sustainable Energy Future**, announced during the 2012 East Asia Summit, is a policy initiative that includes up to $6 billion from federal trade and investment promotion agencies to finance exports and investments related to energy infrastructure in the region.[40] OPIC stated that it will provide up to $1 billion in financing for sustainable power and infrastructure projects in the region, in support of the initiative.[41]
- **Power Africa**, announced by the President in June 2013, is an initiative to double access to power in sub-Saharan Africa. The U.S. government plans to commit more than $7 billion in financial support over the next five years, including up to $1.5 billion in OPIC financing and insurance to energy projects in the region.[42]
- **Look South**, announced in January 2014, is a Department of Commerce-led federal government initiative to help more companies do business with Mexico and the United States' other free trade agreement partners in Latin America. The initiative includes a focus on increasing availability and awareness of investment tools for the region through OPIC.[43]

Budget

Congress directs OPIC to operate "on a self-sustaining basis, taking into account in its financing operations the economic and financial soundness of projects."[44] OPIC's budget is funded from its offsetting collections, which are derived from the premiums, interest, and fees generated from its insurance and finance services and the accumulated interest generated from the agency's investment in U.S. Treasury securities.[45] Its budget is composed of noncredit and credit accounts, in conformity with the standards set out in the Federal Credit Reform Act of 1990 (FCRA). The noncredit portion relates to OPIC's political risk insurance program, while the credit portion is comprised of OPIC's direct and guaranteed loans. OPIC uses premium income and the interest it accrues from the assets in its noncredit account to fund the direct and indirect expenses in its noncredit and credit accounts.

While OPIC has the authority to spend from its own revenue to cover its operations, Congress and the President set OPIC's maximum spending levels for its administrative and program expenses through the annual appropriations process. FY2015 appropriations legislation provided $62.8 million for OPIC's administrative expenses to carry out its credit and insurance programs and authorized a transfer of $25 million from OPIC's noncredit account for the cost of its credit programs (e.g., the cost of modifying loans) (see **Table 3**). The President's FY2016 budget requests $83.5 million for OPIC's administrative expenses to carry out its credit and insurance programs and a transfer of $20 million from its noncredit account for credit program costs.

OPIC has a net negative budget authority; its offsets to budget authority have been greater than its appropriations. According to OPIC, it generated $358 million in "deficit reduction" for the U.S. government in FY2014, representing its 37th consecutive year of generating negative outlays.[46]

OPIC's loan disbursements are financed through two sources: the long-term loan subsidy costs are financed by its collections, and the remaining non-subsidized portion of the loans is financed by borrowings from the Treasury. OPIC finances investment guarantees by issuing certificates of participation in U.S. debt capital markets. OPIC repays the Treasury through collection of loan fees, repayments, and default recoveries. OPIC uses nonbudgetary "financing accounts" to account for credit program cash flow. The subsidy expense for a direct loan or loan guarantee is estimated when it is first disbursed. OPIC reestimates its total subsidy cost at regular intervals based on updated assumptions. Permanent indefinite authority is available to fund any reestimated increase of subsidy costs that occurs after the year in which a loan is disbursed. Reestimated reductions of subsidy costs are returned to the Treasury.[47]

Table 3. OPIC Appropriations, FY2011-FY2016

	FY11	FY12	FY13	FY14	FY15	FY16
Noncredit Account: Administrative expenses ($mn)						
Amount requested	$53.9	$57.9	$60.8	$71.8	$71.8	$83.5
Amount appropriated	$52.3	$54.99	$54.99[a]	$62.6	62.8	---
Credit Account: Program expenses ($mn)						
Amount requested	$29.0	$31.0	$31.0	$31.0	$25.0	$20.0
Amount appropriated	$18.1	$25.0	$25.0[a]	$27.4	$25.0	---
Staff: Direct civilian full-time equivalents	205	220	229	223	280[b]	290[b]

Source: *Budget of the United States Government*, various years, U.S. Government Printing Office, Washington; and appropriations legislation, various years.

Notes:

[a] Data do not reflect sequestration reduction.

[b] Estimated.

Risk Management

OPIC seeks to promote private sector investment in developing and emerging economies through offering financial products that help to mitigate the political and commercial risks of making qualified investments overseas. As such, OPIC faces certain risks in its activities. Congress directs OPIC to "conduct its insurance operations with due regard to the principles of risk management...."[48] OPIC assesses the credit and other risks of proposed transactions; monitors current commitments for risks; and seeks recoveries in instances where it pays or settles valid claims.[49] OPIC also states that it budgets and accounts for risk in its credit portfolio through FCRA. According to OPIC, in FY2014, its credit portfolio had write-offs, net of recoveries, of less than 1%.[50] Additionally, OPIC says that it offsets any potential future losses with reserves (comprised of U.S. Treasury securities).[51] OPIC's cumulative reserves totaled $5.5 billion in FY2014.[52]

In its 43 years of operations, OPIC reports that it has expended more cash than it collected in two fiscal years. Based on its historical record and risk management practices, OPIC recognizes but considers unlikely the possibility, "that a significant credit or insurance event affecting multiple transactions could trigger net losses in [OPIC's] portfolio," resulting in costs exceeding collections in a future fiscal year.[53]

INTERNATIONAL CONTEXT FOR DEVELOPMENT FINANCE

External financial flows to developing countries come through a number of channels. One is official development assistance (ODA) from foreign governments (e.g., grants, concessional lending).[54] Another is private capital flows from foreign companies, including through foreign direct investment (FDI).[55] In developing countries, ODA historically was the main source of external financing. Over time, FDI flows have grown relative to ODA flows (see Figure 3).[56] In the 1990s, FDI flows began outweighing ODA flows in developing countries, and in 2013, they were more than six times greater. Traditionally, FDI largely has flowed from developed countries to developing countries, but emerging markets and developing countries also are becoming significant FDI sources.[57]

Along with the changing international investment landscape, the international development policy landscape has evolved with bilateral and multilateral development financing institutions (DFIs) playing a more active role. DFIs are used here to refer to entities that provide officially backed (or government-backed) support (e.g., through direct loans, loan guarantees, or insurance) for private sector investment in less developed countries.[58]

It is difficult to find centralized, comprehensive sources of information on DFI activities. Officially backed investment financing activities are outside of the scope of the OECD Arrangement on Officially Supported Export Credits, which includes notification procedures and reporting requirements on activity. Countries vary in terms of how much information they publish on their DFI activities. However, according to available estimates, it appears that DFI support has grown relative to ODA in developing countries. For example, based on an estimate by the International Finance Corporation (IFC) using its database, private sector commitments (*not* including political risk insurance) by international financial institutions to developing countries grew from about $10 billion in 2002 to over $40 billion in 2010.[59] A subsequent estimate by the Center for Strategic and International Studies (CSIS), which it said was based on the same set of institutions, pegged that total at about $68 billion in 2013.[60]

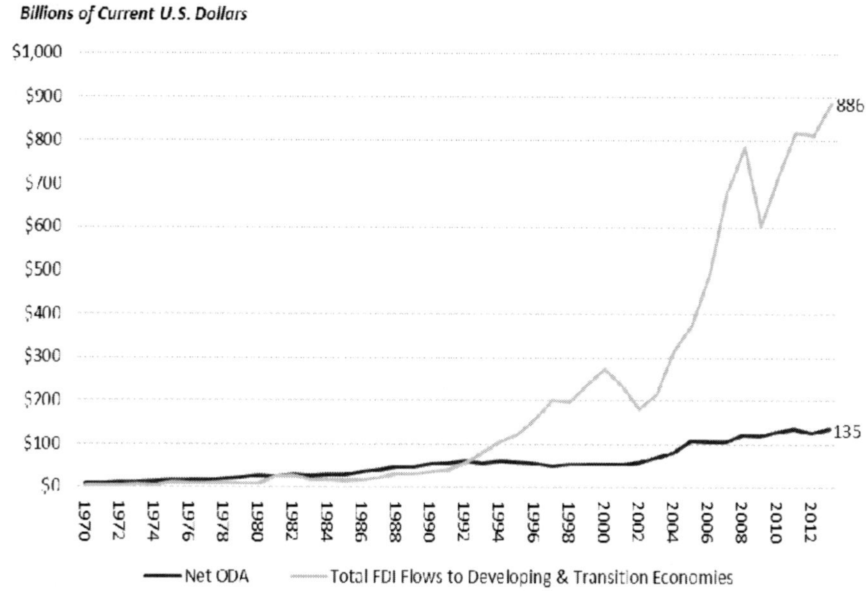

Source: Adapted by CRS. Net ODA data from Organization for Economic Cooperation and Development (OECD), Development Assistance Committee (DAC) table, "Net ODA from DAC countries from 1950 to 2014," http://www.oecd.org/dac/stats/data.htm. FDI data from United Nations Conference on Trade and Development (UNCTAD), UNCTADstat, FDI flows, http://unctad.org/en/Pages/Statistics.aspx.

Figure 3. Net Official Development Assistance (ODA) and Foreign Direct Investment (FDI) Flows to Developing Countries, 1970-2013.

The level of DFI support for the private sector through political risk insurance also may be significant. The Berne Union, an international group of private and state export credit and foreign investment insurers, maintains statistics on political risk insurance provided by its members linked to FDI.[61] However, these data may include investment support *not* related to development finance, given the group's membership. According to the Berne Union, its members' newly underwritten investment insurance transactions reached close to $100 billion in 2014, up from about $66 billion in 2010; and its members' total portfolio of insured investment reached about $238 billion in 2014, up from about $193 billion in 2010.[62]

Table 4. Selected Development Finance Institutions (DFIs)

Development Finance Institutions	Sponsor
Bilateral	
Overseas Private Investment Corporation (OPIC)	United States
Association of European Development Finance Institutions (EDFI)	
Belgian Investment Company for Developing Countries (BIO); Belgian Corporation for International Investment (SBI-BMI)	Belgium
CDCGroup*	United Kingdom
Compañía Española de Financiación del Desarrollo (COFIDES)	Spain
Entrepreneurial Development Cooperation (DEG)	Germany
Finnish Fund for Industrial Cooperation Ltd. (FINNFUND)	Finland
The Investment Fund for Developing Countries (IFU)	Denmark
Netherlands Development Finance Company(FMO)	Netherlands
Norwegian Investment Fund for Developing Countries (Norfund)	Norway
Oesterreichische Entwicklungbank AG (OoEB; The Development Bank of Austria)	Austria
Société de Promotion et de Participation pour la Coopération Economique (Proparco)	France
Swiss Investment Fund for Emerging Markets (SIFEM)	Switzerland
SocietàItaliana per le Imprese all'Estero (SIMEST)	Italy
Sociedade para o Financiamento do Desenvolvimento (SOFID)	Portugal
Swedfund International AB (Swedfund)	Sweden
Japanese Bank for International Cooperation (JBIC)	Japan
Export-Import Bank of China; China Export and Credit Insurance Corporation (Sinosure); China Development Bank (CDB)	China
Brazilian Development Bank (BNDES)	Brazil
Export Credit Guarantee Corporation of India (ECGC)	India
Regional	
African Development Bank (AfDB); Asian Development Bank (ADB); European Bank for Reconstruction and Development (EBRD); Inter-American Development Bank (IDB)	
Multilateral	
International Finance Corporation (IFC)**; Multilateral Investment Guaranty Agency (MIGA)**	

Source: CRS compilation from International Finance Corporation (IFC), *International Finance Institutions and Development: Private Sector*, 2011; Christian Kingombe, Isabella Massa and Dirk Willem te Velde, *Comparing Development Institutions Literature Review*, Overseas Development Institute, January 20, 2011; Association of European Development Finance Institutions (EDFI) publications; and various other DFI publications and annual reports.

Notes: * CDC (United Kingdom) formerly was Colonial Development Corporation, then Commonwealth Development Corporation.

** IFC and MIGA are both part of The World Bank Group.

While developed countries, such as the United States (through OPIC) and some other G-7 countries, traditionally have been the sources of development finance activities, emerging economies such as China, Brazil, and India also have become significant players in this space. Presently, OPIC has many counterparts internationally (see Table 4). The growing number of development finance players and volumes of investment financing have resulted in greater and varied competition for U.S. businesses—competition from firms in both developed countries and from emerging economies as they move up the value chain. U.S. companies may seek OPIC assistance to counter the officially backed investment support that their competitors receive. At the same time, from an economic perspective, the role of government-backed financing and its impact on markets is debated.

Below are some general comparisons of OPIC and selected other DFIs; these comparisons are illustrative of the DFI landscape and not comprehensive.

- **Ownership:** OPIC and certain other DFIs are owned exclusively by the public sector, such as CDC (United Kingdom) and DEG (Germany). Others, such as FMO (the Netherlands) and Proparco (France), have joint public and private ownership. Regional and multilateral DFIs (such as EBRD and IFC) have multiple shareholders from various countries.
- **Organizational Structure:** Countries vary in how they organize their investment and export financing functions. The United States houses investment and export financing functions in separate entities, OPIC (the official U.S. DFI) and the Export-Import Bank of the United States (the official U.S. export credit agency). The two agencies have different missions—with OPIC focused more on foreign policy and development goals and Ex-Im Bank geared toward commercial goals—although they do coordinate on certain transactions. By comparison, some other countries house these functions in the same entity.[63] For example, JBIC (Japan) conducts both investment and export financing operations.
- **International Rules:** As discussed earlier, the investment financing activities of DFIs fall outside of the forms of financing regulated by international disciplines through the OECD Arrangement on Officially Supported Export Credits. The Arrangement includes limitations on financial terms and conditions in areas such as down payments, repayment terms, interest rates and premia, and country

risk classifications. It contains notification procedures and reporting requirements for countries' export credit activities to encourage transparency. Among other things, the Arrangement does *not* apply to investment support not directly linked or tied to procurement from the country providing the official support.[64]

- **Activities:** DFIs provide investment support through a range of financial instruments. OPIC provides investment support through direct loans, loan guarantees, and political risk insurance. In contrast, many other DFIs offer a larger suite of financial products, including participating as a limited partner in private equity funds. According to OPIC, it is the only one of at least 30 private sector-focused DFIs without the ability to participate as a limited partner in private equity funds.[65] For instance, the CDC (United Kingdom); DEG (Germany); FMO (Netherlands); Proparco (France); and IFC (multilateral) reportedly had equity authority as of FY2012.[66] In some cases, equity may be the primary focus of DFI activity. Additionally, some DFIs provide "project-specific and general technical assistance."[67] OPIC provides limited technical support.
- **Portfolio Size:** The size of DFI portfolios varies. For example, OPIC's cumulative portfolio totaled $18 billion in FY2013. In comparison, according to the Association of the European Development Finance Institutions (EDFI), at the end of 2013, its 15 members collectively had a total portfolio of €28 billion (about $39 billion), although each member individually had a portfolio of less than €7 billion (about $10 billion).[68]
- Ex-Im Bank's annual competitiveness report, while focused on export financing, includes some data on investment financing as part of countries' "total official medium- and long-term (MLT) trade-related support." By Ex-Im Bank estimates, OECD members' MLT investment financing totaled $51 billion in 2014, up from $42 billion in 2013, while China's MLT investment financing *alone* totaled $43 billion in 2014, up from $37 billion in 2013.[69] (These data may include investment financing that some would *not* consider as development finance. Also, these data may exclude short-term investment financing that may be included in the above OPIC vs. EDFI comparison.)
- **Portfolio Distribution:** DFIs support projects in a range of economic sectors. Infrastructure and financial services have been major areas of focus, but support for other sectors, such as agribusiness, is also a

focus. For emerging market DFIs, securing access to natural resources is a key focus or related outcome of development finance activities. For example, securing access to natural resources in sub-Saharan Africa is widely regarded as an important motivation for China's investment financing in the region.[70]

- **Policy Requirements:** Requirements that projects must meet in order to receive support vary by DFI, such as with respect to environmental, worker rights, and other conditions. OPIC is widely regarded in the development finance community as having among the most extensive policy requirements for projects to receive its support. According to OPIC, it has been a leader among DFIs in "developing and applying environmental and social policies that advance longterm sustainable development."[71] While some may support such policy goals, others may view the particular requirements stemming from the policies as overly burdensome. In contrast to OPIC, DFIs of emerging market economies, such as China, generally are not considered to have as strong policy requirements, although environmental and other policy considerations may play a factor in their support.

ISSUES FOR CONGRESS

OPIC presents a number of possible issues for Congress, chief of which could be a debate about its reauthorization. As part of the reauthorization process or general oversight of agency, Congress also may examine OPIC's product offerings, policy requirements for supporting projects, activity composition, and organizational structure.

Reauthorization

Congress may examine whether to reauthorize OPIC and, if so, the length of time for which to extend its authority and under what terms. In recent years, Members of Congress have introduced various types of bills concerning OPIC's authority (see text box).

Examples of Bills Related to OPIC's Authority

Some bills have focused exclusively on extending OPIC's authority. For example, in the 112th Congress, two bills were introduced to reauthorize OPIC through FY2015 (H.R.2762 and S.3627).

Other bills have sought to extend OPIC's authority, as well as to make adjustments to OPIC's activity. For instance, in the 111th Congress, S. 705 (Overseas Private Investment Corporation Reauthorization Act of 2009) would have reauthorized OPIC until September 30, 2013. The bill, which was reported out of committee, included provisions related to the transparency and accountability of OPIC's investment funds, OPIC's authority to conduct projects in Iraq, and worker rights. In addition, it included prohibitions on OPIC assistance to entities in countries designated as state sponsors of terrorism.

Bills on other policy issues have included a renewal of OPIC's authority. For example, in the 114th Congress, H.R. 2847 and S. 1933 (both entitled Electrify Africa Act of 2015) would increase U.S. government support, including through OPIC, to assist sub-Saharan African countries in increasing electricity access to support economic growth and other goals. The bills, among other things, would extend OPIC's authority until September 30, 2018.

The debate over reauthorization also could involve congressional consideration of other outcomes, such as privatizing or terminating the functions of OPIC (see "Organizational Structure" discussion further below).

Congressional views differ on the economic and foreign policy rationales for OPIC. One issue is the relationship between OPIC and the private sector.[72] Supporters argue that OPIC fills gaps in private sector political risk insurance and financing for investment and helps "level the playing field" for U.S. businesses competing against foreign companies supported by their own DFIs, while critics argue that OPIC distorts the flow of capital and resources away from efficient uses and crowds out viable, private sector alternatives for investment financing and insurance. Those in favor of OPIC also assert that it provides support for projects, markets, and sectors where government-backed financing and insurance can make the most difference (e.g., large-scale, long-term infrastructure projects, investments by small businesses, projects in developing countries, and during financial crises), while those critical of OPIC point out that the majority of U.S. overseas investments occur without OPIC support and question why OPIC should take on risk when the private sector does not want to.

Other points of debate include the composition of OPIC's activities and its outcomes. Supporters argue that U.S. companies of all sizes benefit from OPIC and that OPIC charges interest, premia, and other fees for its support, while critics contend that OPIC, as a form of government intervention, is "corporate welfare" and that, by dollar value, larger companies are the primary beneficiaries. Supporters note OPIC's risk management practices, low non-performance and high recovery rates, and contributions to the Treasury, while critics express concern about the potential risks that OPIC's activities pose to U.S. taxpayers. Also, supporters argue that OPIC screens projects for "additionality" and that its activities contribute to U.S. jobs and exports, while critics question OPIC's opportunity costs and express concern that OPIC supports companies whose overseas investments may result in the outsourcing of U.S. jobs.

From a foreign policy perspective, supporters contend that OPIC's activities, on a demand-driven basis, advance U.S. development and national security interests by contributing to economic development in poor countries, while critics counter that the actual composition of OPIC's activities may not reflect U.S. foreign policy priorities and that the development benefits of OPIC's activities are questionable.

From an operational standpoint, some argue that OPIC would benefit from multi-year authorizations and "that the potential risk of a lapse undermines the private sector's confidence in OPIC's effectiveness, given that clients and projects require long-term planning and exit horizons."[73] Others argue that shorter extensions may provide opportunity for Congress to weigh in more frequently on OPIC operations through the lawmaking process. Questions may be raised about the extent that yearly renewals of authority through the appropriations process affect OPIC and what issues may be discussed in a broader debate about OPIC's authority.

Congress also may evaluate the impact of a lapse or expiration of OPIC's authority. For instance, OPIC's authority lapsed during April-September 2008. During this period, OPIC was able to disburse funds for already committed projects, but was unable to sign contracts for new projects.[74] This lapse in authority reportedly contributed to a backlog of projects in OPIC's pipeline of, by one estimate, about $2 billion of potential transactions.[75]

Product Offerings

OPIC currently provides political risk insurance, project and investment funds financing through direct loans and loan guarantees, and other services. Of congressional interest may be whether to expand OPIC's product offerings.

Equity Authority

A long-standing topic of debate is whether OPIC should be able to make equity investments in investment funds, in addition to the current debt financing that it provides for such funds.[76]

According to OPIC, it currently does not have resources to make limited partnership investments.[77] OPIC's FY2016 congressional budget justification includes a request for authority to use up to $20 million from its Credit Reform Appropriation and $20 million in transfer authority to invest in private equity funds that serve OPIC's mission.[78] Proponents argue that equity authority would enable OPIC to exert greater influence in an investment's strategic goals and economic, social, and governance policies; that foreign counterparts, many of whom have equity authority,[79] may be more likely to partner with OPIC on projects, increasing OPIC's ability to leverage its resources; and that OPIC could use the higher returns generally associated with equity investments to support more projects. Critics may raise concerns about the U.S. government taking an ownership stake in a private enterprise; the greater resources required for equity investments; and the greater risks and financial exposure associated with equity investments.

Technical Assistance

A point of debate among stakeholders is whether should have OPIC a consistent ability to provide grants, such as for technical assistance, for the projects that it supports. Those in favor of such proposals contend that providing technical assistance would enhance OPIC's effectiveness in supporting projects.[80] On the other hand, critics contend that providing OPIC with a significant grant function would duplicate the roles of USAID and the TDA in development assistance.

Policies

In supporting U.S. private sector investment overseas, OPIC seeks to balance multiple policy objectives, including foreign assistance, development, economic, environmental, and other policy goals. Congress could evaluate how OPIC might prioritize and balance these various objectives.

OPIC's Environmental Policy and Recent Developments

Based on FY2010 appropriations language (P.L. 111-117, §7079(b)) as well as other factors, OPIC has engaged in efforts to reduce the direct greenhouse gas (GHG) emissions associated with projects in its active portfolio (i.e., all insurance contracts in force and all guaranty and direct loans with an outstanding principal balance) by 30% over a 10 year period (June 30, 2008-September 30, 2018) and by 50% over a 15-year period (June 30, 2008-September 30, 2023).[81]

FY2015 appropriations language (P.L. 113-235, §7086(4)) includes a provision that would prohibit the use of OPIC funds, until September 30, 2014, and under certain conditions, for the enforcement of any rule or guideline implementing: (1) OPIC's GHG reductions policy; or (2) OPIC's proposed modification to its Environmental and Social Policy Statement (ESPS) related to coal.[82] Under the appropriations language, the use of appropriated funds by OPIC to implement the GHG emissions reduction policy and proposed coal-related modification to the ESPS would not be allowed *if* their implementation would prohibit (or have the effect of prohibiting) any coal-fired or other power-generation projects that satisfy *two* conditions: (1) the purpose of the project is to "provide affordable electricity in International Development Association (IDA)-eligible countries and IDA-blend countries"[83]; *and* (2) the purpose of the project is to "increase exports of goods and services from the United States or to prevent the loss of jobs from the United States." FY2014 appropriations language (P.L. 113-76, §7081(4)) also included this prohibition.

One outcome of the appropriations language is potentially increased opportunities for greater OPIC support for overseas coal-related projects in developing countries. Some stakeholders may argue that the appropriations language provides greater flexibility for OPIC to more effectively meet its development mandate and, in turn, support U.S. jobs and growth. Others may be critical of the language from an environmental perspective.

OPIC's environmental policies on greenhouse gas (GHG) emission reductions (referred to by some stakeholders as a "carbon cap"), in particular, have been the subject of congressional action and vigorous stakeholder debate (see **text box**). On one hand, such efforts may serve U.S. environmental policy goals and help to improve the sustainability of OPIC's activities. On the other hand, some U.S. businesses argue that the GHG emissions reduction effort can constrain their ability to utilize OPIC support and place them at a competitive disadvantage vis-à-vis foreign firms when competing for international project contracts (e.g., major infrastructure projects in sub-Saharan Africa). Other DFIs generally do not have the same level of policy restrictions that OPIC has, potentially enabling them to support a broader array of energy-related projects. From a development perspective, some argue that the GHG emission reduction effort prevents OPIC from supporting projects likely to have the largest development impact.

Activity Areas

One area of congressional interest could be whether OPIC's portfolio has an appropriate mix in terms of its development objectives. Some analysts and stakeholders, for example, have expressed concern about what they see as movement away from projects in sectors commonly viewed as contributing to poverty reduction (e.g., agriculture, infrastructure, and transportation) and toward projects in other sectors where development benefits may be less clear (e.g., finance and hotels). Drivers of such trends may have been environmental policies constraining support for large-scale infrastructure projects, as well as the need to balance financial risks and be self-sustaining. Congressional concern was voiced, for example, about OPIC's support for projects that do not necessarily, on their face, appear to align with OPIC's development mission, such as the construction of a shopping mall in Jordan, expanded billboard advertising in Ukraine, and hotels in Armenia and Georgia.[84] Others may counter that OPIC conducts development impact assessments of proposed projects and monitors the development impact of existing projects; they also may point to the development impacts of projects discussed in OPIC's annual policy reports, for instance in terms of host country employment.[85]

Another area of congressional interest could be considering opportunities for enhancing OPIC's support for specific geographical regions, countries, or sectors that are of U.S. policy priority. For example, some Members, business groups, and other stakeholders assert that there is potential for greater support by OPIC for U.S. investment in Africa. Proposals have included providing additional federal resources to support OPIC investment promotion activity in Africa and/or directing OPIC and other federal agencies to dedicate designated amounts of financing and personnel to foster greater U.S. investment in

Africa.[86] On one hand, greater resources may increase capacity to promote investment, but on the other hand, federal agencies' allocation of funds for trade and investment promotion is generally demand-driven. Thus, for example, if U.S. firms do not seek such assistance due to lack of sufficient commercial interest, such funds may not be fully tapped. At the same time, promotion of development finance opportunities by OPIC could motivate U.S. companies to become more engaged.

Organizational Structure

Congress may wish to examine OPIC's organizational structure and oversight in terms of the agency's effectiveness and efficiency in fulfilling its mandate. What follows are three possible areas of consideration.

- **Reorganization:** Congress could consider merging OPIC with other federal agencies as part of broader reorganization proposals. For example, in 2012, the President proposed reorganizing the business- and trade-related functions of OPIC and five other federal entities into one department to streamline the federal government and make it more effective.[87] The President reiterated the proposal in his FY2016 budget request.[88] Other proposals offered by stakeholders include consolidating federal agencies focused on promoting international development through private sector tools (such as OPIC, TDA, and certain elements of USAID) and consolidating federal trade finance agencies (such as OPIC and the Ex-Im Bank).[89] While reorganization prospects in the near term are unclear, the renewed focus has rekindled policy debates about whether reorganization would reduce costs and improve the effectiveness of trade policy programs, or undermine the effectiveness of federal agencies, given their differing missions.[90]
- **Privatization or Termination:** Congress could consider privatizing or terminating OPIC, the feasibility of which previously has been analyzed.[91] Supporters of such options may argue that OPIC's self-sustaining nature is proof that there is no market failure; that OPIC competes with or crowds out the private sector, which is more efficient and better suited than the federal government to support investments; and that OPIC's activities impose potential costs and risks on U.S. taxpayers, since they are backed by the full faith and

credit of the U.S. government.[92] Those in favor of OPIC may argue that the federal government plays a unique role in addressing market failures; that OPIC's backing by the full faith and credit of the U.S. government may make certain transactions more commercially attractive or give OPIC leverage to guarantee repayment in a way that is not available to the private sector; and that federal investment support is critical when there is a shortfall in private sector financing and insurance.

- **Internal Oversight:** Congress could examine OPIC's own internal oversight structure. Presently, USAID's Inspector General has legal authority to conduct reviews, investigations, and inspections of OPIC's operations and activities,[93] while external auditors conduct audits of OPIC's financial statements and report findings to OPIC's Board of Directors.[94] One possibility is establishing an OPICspecific Inspector General.[95] Some may support this approach given differences in OPIC's private sector financing focus and USAID's grant-making functions. Opponents may assert that the current OPIC-USAID arrangement suffices or express concern about the additional resources a new Inspector General could require. Other possibilities include directing Ex-Im Bank's Inspector General to conduct OPIC oversight. Some may support this on the basis that Ex-Im Bank and OPIC offer some similar financing and insurance products, though others may express concern because of differences in the two agencies' missions and stakeholders.

End Notes

[1] For additional information, see OPIC's website: http://www.opic.gov/.

[2] As used in this report, the term DFI refers to an entity that provides officially backed (or government-backed) support (e.g., through direct loans, loan guarantees, or insurance) for private sector investment in developing countries. Development finance also can take place by other means that do not directly involve supporting the private sector. For example, the World Bank Group's International Bank for Reconstruction and Development (IBRD) and International Development Association (IDA) provide financial support to middle- and/or low-income governments for development purposes. For more information, see CRS Report R41170, *Multilateral Development Banks: Overview and Issues for Congress*, by Rebecca M. Nelson. As another example, the U.S. Agency for International Development (USAID) supports activities in developing countries working through recipient country governments and non-governmental organizations, rather than directly with private investors. However,

within the OPIC context, the term DFI generally refers to the involvement of the private sector.

[3] 22 U.S.C. §2191 *et seq.*

[4] 22 U.S.C. §2195(a)(2).

[5] §7073(b) of the FY2015 appropriations act (P.L. 113-235) states, "Notwithstanding section 235(a)(2) of the Foreign Assistance Act of 1961 [which states the expiration date for OPIC's authority], the authority of subsections (a) through (c) of section 234 of such Act [i.e., investment insurance, investment guarantees, and direct insurance] shall remain in effect until September 30, 2015."

[6] 22 U.S.C. §2191.

[7] U.S. Congress, House Committee on Foreign Affairs, Subcommittee on Terrorism, Nonproliferation, and Trade, *Testimony by Elizabeth Littlefield, President and CEO, OPIC*, Hearing on "Trade Promotion Agencies and U.S. Foreign Policy," 114th Cong., 1st sess., May 19, 2015.

[8] For example, OPIC is a part of the interagency Trade Promotion Coordinating Committee (TPCC) and the President's Export Promotion Cabinet; participated in the National Export Initiative (NEI), President Obama's plan to grow U.S. exports; and is participating in the NEI's successor, NEI/NEXT.

[9] *Public Papers of the Presidents: Richard Nixon*, Washington, U.S. Government Printing Office, 1969, p. 412.

[10] More generally, U.S. foreign assistance continues to evolve. See CRS Report R40213, *Foreign Aid: An Introduction to U.S. Programs and Policy*, by Curt Tarnoff and Marian L. Lawson.

[11] The role that OPIC plays in mitigating risks of investing overseas has some parallels to protections offered to investors under U.S. international investment agreements (IIAs), which commonly take the form of bilateral investment treaties (BITs) and investment chapters of free trade agreements (FTAs). For more information, see CRS Report R44015, *International Investment Agreements (IIAs): Frequently Asked Questions*, coordinated by Martin A. Weiss.

[12] OPIC, "Political Risk Insurance," https://www.opic.gov/what-we-offer/political-risk-insurance.

[13] OPIC, "Financial Products," https://www.opic.gov/what-we-offer/financial-products.

[14] OPIC, "Enterprise Development Network," http://www.opic.gov/doing-business/edn.

[15] OPIC, "Investment Funds," http://www.opic.gov/what-we-offer/investment-funds.

[16] U.S. General Accounting Office (now General Accountability Office, GAO), *Overseas Investment: The Overseas Private Investment Corporation's Investment Funds Program*, GAO/NSIAD-00-159BR, May 2000, http://www.gao.gov/assets/80/79265.pdf.

[17] Ibid.

[18] OPIC, "*Expanding Horizons*," http://www.opic.gov/media-connections/events-speakers/expanding-horizons.

[19] According to the OECD, an ECA is an "agency in a creditor country that provides insurance, guarantees, or loans for the export of goods and services." ECA activities may be in low-income countries but generally do not have development-related objectives, although they may have a development impact. See Kaori Miyamoto and Kim Biousse, *Official Support for Private Sector Participation in Developing Country Infrastructure*, OECD, OECD Development Co-operation Working Papers No. 19, 2014, p. 16, http://www.oecd-ilibrary.org/development/official-support-forprivate-sector-participation-in-developing-country-infrastructure_5jz14cd40nf0-en.

[20] The role of the OECD Arrangement is to help "level the playing field" so that decisions to purchase goods and services are based on price and quality, rather than financing terms. See

CRS Report R43671, *Export-Import Bank Reauthorization: Frequently Asked Questions*, coordinated by Shayerah Ilias Akhtar; and CRS Report IF10017, *Export-Import Bank (Ex-Im Bank) Reauthorization*, by Shayerah Ilias Akhtar.

[21] Ex-Im Bank, *Report the U.S. Congress on Export Credit Competition and the Export-Import Bank of the United States*, for the period January 1, 2014 through December 31, 2014, June 2015, p. 7, http://www.exim.gov/sites/default/files/reports/EXIM% 202014CompetReport_0611.pdf.

[22] 22 U.S.C. §2195(a). OPIC's exposure "includes undisbursed commitments (obligations) and maximum contingent liability under OPIC's current insurance contracts." *Annual Management Report of the Overseas Private Investment Corporation for Fiscal Year 2014*, p. 5, https://www.opic.gov/sites/default/files/files/opic-financials-0302.pdf.

[23] *OPIC 2014 Annual Report*, p. 4, https://www.opic.gov/sites/default/files/files/opic-fy14-annual-report.pdf.

[24] CRS calculation based on data in *OPIC 2000 Annual Report*, pp. 33-34, https://www.opic.gov/sites/default/files/docs/00_AnnualReport.pdf.

[25] CRS calculation based on data in *Annual Management Report of the Overseas Private Investment Corporation for Fiscal Year 2014*, p. 9.

[26] *OPIC 2014 Annual Report,* p. 4; and OPIC, *Congressional Budget Justification – Fiscal Year 2016*, p. 15, https://www.opic.gov/sites/default/files/files/20150309-opic-cbj-final.pdf.

[27] OPIC, *Congressional Budget Justification – Fiscal Year 2016*, p. 15; and *OPIC 2014 Annual Report,* p. 5.

[28] Discussion draws from OPIC annual reports, congressional budget justifications, and press releases.

[29] According to OPIC, "[f]rom time to time, statutory and policy constraints may limit the availability of OPIC programs in certain countries, or countries where programs were previously unavailable may become eligible." For example, OPIC suspended its programs in China following the 1989 crackdown on Tiananmen Square protestors. Department of State, *2013 Investment Climate Statement China*, February 2013, http://www.state.gov/e/eb/rls/othr/ics/2013/204621.htm.

[30] *OPIC 2014 Annual Report,* p. 5.

[31] U.S. Congress, Senate Committee on Foreign Relations, *Hearing on Power Africa Initiative*, Testimony of Mimi Alemayehou, Executive Vice President, OPIC, 113th Cong., 2nd sess., March 26, 2014; and *2014 OPIC Annual Report*, p. 3.

[32] OPIC, *Congressional Budget Justification – Fiscal Year 2012*, pp. 5-6, https://www.opic.gov/sites/default/files/files/opic-fy12-cbj.pdf. OPIC defines impact investing as "investments in businesses that are designed with the intent to generate positive social and/or environmental impact" and "can include business sectors such as basic needs (food, water, sanitation, housing), basic services (education, health care, clean technology), and financial services (microfinance and small and medium enterprise finance)."

[33] *2014 OPIC Annual Report*, p. 4.

[34] OPIC, *Congressional Budget Justification – Fiscal Year 2016*, p. 11.

[35] *2014 OPIC Annual Report*, p. 19.

[36] OPIC, "OPIC to Provide Up to $2 Billion for Investment in Middle East and North Africa," press release, March 11, 2011, https://www.opic.gov/press-releases/2011/opic-provide-2-billion-investment-middle-east-and-north-africa.

[37] Office of the Press Secretary, "Remarks by the President on the Middle East and North Africa," The White House, State Department, Washington, DC, May 19, 2011,

http://www.whitehouse.gov/the-press-office/2011/05/19/remarkspresident-middle-east-and-north-africa.

[38] OPIC, "OPIC Board Approves $500 Million for Small Business Lending in Egypt and Jordan," press release, July 1, 2011, http://www.opic.gov/news/press-releases/2009/pr070111.

[39] John Morton, "U.S.-Africa Clean Energy Finance Initiative – Supporting renewable energy to power Africa," OPIC, blog, January 13, 2015, https://www.opic.gov/blog/renewables/u-s-africa-clean-energy-finance-initiative-supportingrenewable-energy-to-power-africa; and U.S. Diplomatic Mission to South Africa, "OPIC to dedicate staff member for South Africa in 2013," press release, October 16, 2012, http://southafrica.usembassy.gov/press_121017a.html.

[40] The White House, "Fact Sheet on the U.S.-Asia Pacific Comprehensive Partnership for a Sustainable Energy," press release, November 20, 2012, http://www.whitehouse.gov/the-press-office/2012/11/20/fact-sheet-us-asia-pacificcomprehensive-partnership-sustainable-energy.

[41] OPIC, *Congressional Budget Justification – Fiscal Year 2016*, p. 16.

[42] The White House, "Fact Sheet: Power Africa," press release, June 30, 2013, http://www.whitehouse.gov/the-pressoffice/2013/06/30/fact-sheet-power-africa.

[43] Department of Commerce, "Fact Sheet: Look South Initiative," January 9, 2014, http://www.commerce.gov/news/fact-sheets/2014/01/fact-sheet-look-south-initiative.

[44] 22 U.S.C. §2191(a).

[45] Prior to FY1992, OPIC relied exclusively on resources controlled outside the annual appropriations process (fees and interest on Treasury securities) to fund its operations. With federal government credit reform, however, OPIC was required to receive an appropriation based on an estimate of its credit programs (direct loans and guarantees). From 1992 to 1994, OPIC received an appropriation to cover its operations from the General Fund of the U.S. Treasury and reimbursed the amount of that appropriation from its collections. For FY1998 and beyond, OPIC's appropriations language provides OPIC with the authority to spend their own collections, without the need for a General Fund appropriation.

[46] OPIC, *Congressional Budget Justification – Fiscal Year 2016*, p. 5. This amount is on a cash basis, and is different than the amount calculated on a budgetary basis.

[47] OPIC, "Financial Products," https://www.opic.gov/what-we-offer/financial-products/products. See also *Annual Management Report of the Overseas Private Investment Corporation for Fiscal Year 2014*, pp. 23-26.

[48] 22 U.S.C. §2191(d).

[49] For more information, see OPIC, *2014 Annual Claims Report*, September 30, 2014, https://www.opic.gov/sites/default/files/files/2014%20Annual%20Claims%20Report.pdf.

[50] OPIC, "OPIC Achieves $3 Billion in Commitments for 2014, Catalyzing Billions More, While Supporting American Business Growth in Developing Countries," press release, December 18, 2014, https://www.opic.gov/press-releases/2014/opic-achieves-3-billion-commitments-2014-catalyzing-billions-more-while-supporting-american-business-growth-.

[51] *Annual Management Report of the Overseas Private Investment Corporation for Fiscal Year 2014*, p. 5.

[52] Ibid.

[53] Ibid.

[54] See OECD, Development Co-operation Directorate (DCD-DAC), http://www.oecd.org/dac/stats/data.htm.

[55] Foreign direct investment (FDI) takes place when a resident (including a company) of one country obtains a lasting interest in, and a degree of influence over the management of, a business enterprise in another country.

[56] Official development assistance (ODA), as defined and reported by the OECD, differs from U.S. government measures of foreign assistance because it excludes all military assistance and assistance to developed countries, among other things. For more information, see CRS Report R40213, *Foreign Aid: An Introduction to U.S. Programs and Policy*, by Curt Tarnoff and Marian L. Lawson.

[57] For background, see United Nations Conference on Trade and Development (UNCTAD), *World Investment Report 2015 – Reforming International Investment Governance*, http://unctad.org/en/pages/PublicationWebflyer.aspx?publicationid=1245.

[58] Development finance can take place through other means that do not directly involve supporting the private sector. For example, the World Bank Group's International Bank for Reconstruction and Development (IBRD) and International Development Association (IDA) provide financial support to middle- and/or low-income governments for development purposes. For more information, see CRS Report R41170, *Multilateral Development Banks: Overview and Issues for Congress*, by Rebecca M. Nelson. As another example, USAID supports activities in developing countries working through recipient country governments and non-governmental organizations, rather than directly with private investors.

[59] According to the International Finance Corporation (IFC), it is estimated that over 90% of private sector finance by international financial institutions is covered in its database. IFC, *International Finance Institutions and Development Through the Private Sector*, A joint report of 31 multilateral and bilateral development finance institutions, 2011, p. 36, http://www.developmentandtheprivatesector.org/.

[60] Daniel F. Runde and Helen Moser, *DFI Finance Increases to One Half of ODA*, CSIS, July 13, 2015, http://csis.org/publication/dfi-finance-increases-one-half-oda.

[61] The Berne Union has over 70 member companies (including the Berne Union Prague Club). OPIC and Ex-Im Bank are both members of the Berne Union. For more information, see http://www.berneunion.org/about-the-berne-union/.

[62] Berne Union, *Statistics 2010-2014*, June 24, 2015 (updated), http://www.berneunion.org/wp-content/uploads/2012/10/Berne-Union-2014-Total-and-Complete.pdf.

[63] Entities where investment and export financing functions are combined can variously be called, in some cases, either DFIs or export credit agencies (ECAs).

[64] Ex-Im Bank, *Report the U.S. Congress on Export Credit Competition and the Export-Import Bank of the United States*, for the period January 1, 2014 through December 31, 2014, June 2015, p. 7, http://www.exim.gov/sites/default/files/reports/EXIM%202014 Compet Report_0611.pdf.

[65] OPIC, *Congressional Budget Justification – Fiscal Year 2016*, p. 9.

[66] U.S. Congress, House Committee on Foreign Affairs, Subcommittee on Terrorism, Nonproliferation, and Trade, *Testimony by Elizabeth Littlefield, President and CEO, OPIC*, Hearing on "Trade Promotion Agencies and U.S. Foreign Policy," 114th Cong., 1st sess., May 19, 2015, p. 12.

[67] Daniel F. Runde et al., *Sharing Risk in a World of Danger and Opportunities: Strengthening U.S. Development Finance Capabilities*, Center for Strategic and International Studies (CSIS), December 2011, http://csis.org/files/publication/111205__Runde_SharingRisk_Web.pdf. In the United States, other agencies, such as TDA, provide technical assistance for development projects.

[68] Based on Federal Reserve exchange rate of 1 euro to 1.3779 U.S. dollars on December 31, 2013, accessed on august 20, 2015.

[69] Ex-Im Bank, *Report the U.S. Congress on Export Credit Competition and the Export-Import Bank of the United States*, for the period January 1, 2014 through December 31, 2014, June 2015, pp. 17, 19.

[70] For example, see GAO, *Sub-Saharan Africa: Trends in U.S. and Chinese Economic Engagement*, GAO-13-199, February 2013.

[71] See Appendix 1 of OPIC, *Overseas Private Investment Corporation 2012 Strategic Sustainability Plan,* November 16, 2012, http://www.opic.gov/sites/default/files/files/OPIC_Strategic_Sustainability_Plan_2012.pdf.

[72] For differing views on OPIC, see, for example; Theodore H. Moran, *Reforming OPIC for the 21st Century*, Peterson Institute for International Economics, Policy Analyses in International Economics 69, May 2003; Benjamin Leo, Todd Moss, and Beth Schwanke, *OPIC Unleashed: Strengthening US Tolls to Promote Private-Sector Development Overseas*, Center for Global Development, August 2013, http://www.cgdev.org/sites/default/files/OPIC-Unleashedfinal.pdf; Ian Vasquez and John Welborn, *Reauthorize or Retire the Overseas Private Investment Corporation?*, CATO Institute, Foreign Policy Briefing No. 78, September 15, 2003, http://www.cato.org/publications/foreign-policy-briefing/reauthorize-or-retire-overseas-private-investment-corporation.

[73] Daniel F. Runde et al., *Sharing Risk in a World of Danger and Opportunities: Strengthening U.S. Development Finance Capabilities*, CSIS, December 2011, pp. 5-6.

[74] OPIC, *Congressional Budget Justification – Fiscal Year 2009*, p. iii.

[75] Daniel F. Runde et al., *Sharing Risk in a World of Danger and Opportunities: Strengthening U.S. Development Finance Capabilities*, CSIS, December 2011, p. 5.

[76] OPIC's enabling legislation provides it authority to establish a four-year pilot program under which it may make equity investments in projects in sub-Saharan Africa and in certain "Caribbean basin" countries (specified in 22 U.S.C. §2702) and marine transportation projects, subject to certain limitations and criteria. 22 U.S.C. §2194(g).

[77] OPIC, *Congressional Budget Justification – Fiscal Year 2016*, p. 8.

[78] Ibid.

[79] OPIC, *Congressional Budget Justification – Fiscal Year 2016*, p. 9; and U.S. Congress, House Committee on Foreign Affairs, Subcommittee on Terrorism, Nonproliferation, and Trade, *Testimony by Elizabeth Littlefield, President and CEO, OPIC*, Hearing on "Trade Promotion Agencies and U.S. Foreign Policy," 114th Cong., 1st sess., May 19, 2015, p. 12.

[80] For example, see Daniel F. Runde and Ashley Chandler, *Making the Case for OPIC*, CSIS, May 12, 2011, http://csis.org/publication/making-case-opic; and Benjamin Leo, Todd Moss, and Beth Schwanke, *OPIC Unleashed: Strengthening US Tools to Promote Private-Sector Development Overseas*, CGD, August 2013.

[81] OPIC, *OPIC – Environmental and Social Policy Statement*, October 15, 2010, p. 26.

[82] OPIC's proposed changes are available at: http://www.opic.gov/sites/default/files/files/eisa-changes-policy.pdf.

[83] For more information, see IDA, "IDA Borrowing Countries," http://www.worldbank.org/ida/borrowingcountries.html.

[84] "McCaskill Seeks Greater Oversight of OPIC, TDA; Questions Funding Food Chains, Hotels," *Bloomberg BNA International Trade Daily*, December 13, 2013.

[85] For example, see OPIC, *Annual Report on Development Impact – Fiscal Year 2013*, https://www.opic.gov/sites/default/files/files/report_final_9242014(1).pdf.

[86] See for example, in the 114th Congress,H.R. 1103.

[87] The White House, Office of the Press Secretary, "Government Reorganization Fact Sheet," press release, January 13, 2012, http://www.whitehouse.gov/the-press-office/2012/01/13/government-reorganization-fact-sheet.

[88] OMB, *Budget of the United States Government, Fiscal Year 2016*, "A Government of the Future," p. 81.

[89] For example, see Ben Leo and Todd Moss, *Bringing US Development Finance into the 21st Century*, Center for Global Development, July 20, 2015, http://www.cgdev.org/publication/ft/bringing-us-development-finance-21stcentury-0.

[90] CRS Report R42555, *Trade Reorganization: Overview and Issues for Congress*, by Shayerah Ilias Akhtar.

[91] For example, see J.P. Morgan Securities, Inc., *Overseas Private Investment Corporation: Final Report on the Feasibility of Privatization*, New York, February 7, 1996, cited in GAO, *Overseas Investment: Issues Related to the Overseas Private Investment Corporation's Reauthorization*, GAO/NSIAD-97-230, September 1997, p. 24, http://www.gao.gov/archive/1997/ns97230.pdf.

[92] For example, see Bryan Riley and Brett D. Schaefer, *Time to Privatize OPIC*, The Heritage Foundation, May 19, 2014, http://www.heritage.org/research/reports/2014/05/time-to-privatize-opic.

[93] 22 U.S.C. §2199(e).

[94] 22 U.S.C. §2199(c).

[95] See, for example, H.R. 2847 and S. 1933, introduced in the 114th Congress.

In: The Overseas Private Investment Corporation ISBN: 978-1-63485-728-4
Editor: Molly H. Walsh

Chapter 2

OVERSEAS PRIVATE INVESTMENT CORPORATION: ADDITIONAL ACTIONS COULD IMPROVE MONITORING PROCESSES*

United States Government Accountability Office

WHY GAO DID THIS STUDY

OPIC helps mobilize private capital to address development challenges globally and advance U.S. development assistance objectives.

GAO was asked to provide information on OPIC's financing commitments and its project selection and monitoring practices. This report examines (1) the amounts and types of OPIC financing support for fiscal years 2008 through 2014, (2) how OPIC selects projects, and (3) how OPIC monitors projects.

To address these objectives, GAO analyzed OPIC data for its commitments made in fiscal years 2008 through 2014, to reflect recent activity. GAO also reviewed OPIC policies, annual reports, and selection and monitoring documents for a nongeneralizable sample of 21 projects in four countries. The country and project selections were based on several factors, including OPIC financing amounts, ease of doing business ratings, and project

---

* This is an edited, reformatted and augmented version of the United States Government Accountability Office publication, GAO-16-64, dated December 2015.

sector. GAO interviewed officials from OPIC and other organizations as well as officials and clients in Honduras and Pakistan, two countries with particularly challenging business climates.

What GAO Recommends

GAO recommends that OPIC (1) establish time frames for submitting site visit reports and (2) assess its monitoring processes to ensure risks associated with current practices are acceptable for meeting OPIC's program goals. OPIC concurred with these recommendations.

What GAO Found

The Overseas Private Investment Corporation (OPIC) provides loans, loan guarantees, and political risk insurance to private entities to support development in over 150 countries. In fiscal years 2008 through 2014, OPIC made 718 commitments worldwide valued at about $20 billion. OPIC committed the majority of this financing support to projects in Latin America and the Caribbean and in Sub-Saharan Africa, and 25 percent to countries with low per capita incomes.

OPIC has policies to guide its project selection process, including confirming a connection to the United States and reviewing potential environmental and social, worker rights, and human rights impacts. In its review of a nongeneralizable sample of projects, GAO found that OPIC generally followed these policies. While GAO found that OPIC completed required human rights reviews, the responsibility for reviewing human rights-related information is spread across groups, and OPIC lacked clear guidance for conducting these reviews. OPIC recently developed new guidance that identifies roles and responsibilities for these reviews. GAO also found that OPIC has recently adopted additional guidelines which may support more systematic cumulative environmental and social impact analyses.

OPIC monitors ongoing projects but may lack adequate information about some projects' policy compliance and impacts. OPIC uses annual client-reported data, a limited number of site visits, and independent consultant reports, among other things, to monitor projects' policy compliance and impacts. OPIC policy does not designate time frames for submitting site visit reports, and some reports GAO reviewed were written several years after the visits. OPIC's policy teams visit about one-tenth of active projects each year. Site visit reports GAO reviewed identified compliance issues that clients had not reported, indicating that OPIC may lack complete and accurate information on the status of some projects. Thus, OPIC's current monitoring processes may not provide adequate information on projects' annual policy compliance and development impact status to support program goals.

ABBREVIATIONS

CEO	chief executive officer
IFC	International Finance Corporation
OIP	Office of Investment Policy
OPIC	Overseas Private Investment Corporation
SMQ	self-monitoring questionnaire
State	Department of State
Treasury	Department of the Treasury
USAID	U.S. Agency for International Development
USTR	Office of the U.S. Trade Representative

***

December 11, 2015

The Honorable Edward R. Royce
Chairman
The Honorable Eliot L. Engel
Ranking Member
Committee on Foreign Affairs
House of Representatives

The Honorable Jeff Duncan
Chairman
Subcommittee on the Western Hemisphere
Committee on Foreign Affairs
House of Representatives

The Overseas Private Investment Corporation (OPIC) is the U.S. government's development finance institution, created to complement U.S. development assistance objectives by mobilizing private capital to address development challenges around the world. Much of OPIC's financing support has been for projects in countries with challenging business environments, often lacking adequate infrastructure and effective governance. For example, 54 percent of OPIC's commitments,[1] during fiscal years 2008 through 2014, were in countries ranked in the lower half of the World Bank's ease of doing business index.[2] In 2003, Congress passed legislation reauthorizing OPIC through November 1, 2007.[3] Since then, Congress has extended OPIC's authority to issue political risk insurance and loan guarantees and to make direct loans through annual appropriations for varying periods of time, in no more than 1-year increments.

You asked us to provide information on OPIC's project selection and monitoring practices. This report examines (1) the amounts and types of OPIC's global financing support from fiscal year 2008 through fiscal year 2014, (2) how OPIC selects projects, and (3) how OPIC monitors projects.

To address these objectives, we reviewed OPIC documents and project files and interviewed OPIC staff as well as officials from other U.S. agencies that participate with OPIC in approving projects as members of OPIC's Board of Directors, including the Departments of State (State) and the Treasury (Treasury); the Office of the U.S. Trade Representative (USTR); and the U.S. Agency for International Development (USAID). We also met with officials from the World Bank, including the International Finance Corporation (IFC). We analyzed OPIC-provided data for new commitments it made in fiscal years 2008 through 2014 to characterize OPIC's recent financing support. To assess the reliability of the OPIC- provided data and to better understand the classifications and sources used in its compilation, we interviewed OPIC officials concerning the collection, maintenance, and accuracy of these data. We also performed electronic data testing. We determined that the data were reliable for our purpose, which was to analyze OPIC's new commitments for background and context. We reviewed documents for a nongeneralizable sample of 21 projects in four countries where OPIC has supported investments since 2008—Honduras, Kenya, Pakistan, and Peru. We selected these countries based on factors including OPIC's commitment amounts, diversity of project sectors, geographical coverage, and ease of doing business index ratings. From these countries, we selected a nongeneralizable sample of OPIC projects based on (1) size relative to the total OPIC commitments in the country; (2) sector; (3) type of financing instrument; (4) age of the commitment; and (5) whether any disbursements had been made. To guide our review and analysis of OPIC's project selection and monitoring processes, we created two data collection instruments. In addition, we conducted fieldwork in Honduras and Pakistan, where we visited project sites and interviewed U.S. embassy officials, host-government officials, recipients of OPIC loans and loan guarantees, and officials from other development finance institutions. We did not review the sufficiency of OPIC's credit and legal due diligence processes or OPIC's processes for monitoring projects' financial performance. For additional information concerning our scope and methodology, see appendix I.

We conducted this performance audit from December 2014 to December 2015 in accordance with generally accepted government auditing standards. Those standards require that we plan and perform the audit to obtain sufficient, appropriate evidence to provide a reasonable basis for our findings and conclusions based on our audit objectives. We believe that the evidence obtained provides a reasonable basis for our findings and conclusions based on our audit objectives.

BACKGROUND

OPIC's Financing Seeks to Promote Development and Other Policy Goals by Supporting U.S. Investment Abroad

OPIC, a U.S. government agency under the policy guidance of the Secretary of State, provides financing support to promote development and other policy goals by supporting U.S. direct investment in over 150 countries, with a mandate to give priority to low-income and emerging economies. OPIC's direct loans, loan guaranties, political risk insurance, and private equity investment funds promote U.S. private investment by mitigating risks for U.S. firms making qualified investments overseas, often in difficult business environments. Since it began operating in 1971, OPIC has supported more than $200 billion of U.S. private investment. Examples of OPIC-supported projects include solar and wind power, financing for affordable housing, investments in affordable healthcare, microfinance, agriculture, and manufacturing (see figure 1).

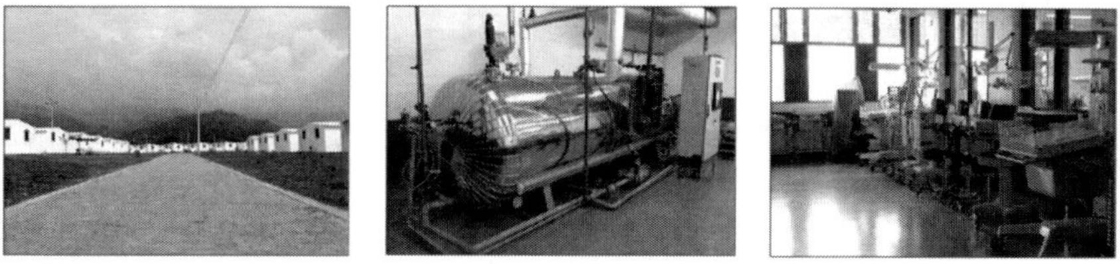

An OPIC direct loan helped fund this low-income housing project in the Sula Valley of Honduras.

This food processing equipment at a plant in Honduras was financed through OPIC-guaranteed loans.

An OPIC direct loan helped fund an expansion to this medical health care facility in Pakistan.

Source: GAO (photos). | GAO-16-64

Figure 1. Examples of Overseas Private Investment Corporation (OPIC) Projects.

OPIC is self-sustaining, and is required by law to hold its revenues and income in order to pay OPIC expenses, cover transfers and additions to the insurance and guaranty reserves, and pay dividends. For example, it uses revenues from fees charged to clients, interest, and insurance premiums and interest earned on the U.S. Treasury securities it holds to cover its operating cost and any program losses.[4] OPIC's maximum spending levels for administrative and program expenses are set annually by Congress. In each of fiscal years 2014 and 2015, Congress authorized approximately $63 million for OPIC's administrative expenses. OPIC is authorized by law to incur up to $29 billion in maximum contingent liability—the amount OPIC would incur if claims were made on all insurance contracts and borrowers defaulted on all loans.[5]

As of September 30, 2015, OPIC's outstanding financial commitments—the value of its portfolio—were approximately $19.9 billion, which is slightly more than two-thirds of its legislated limit of $29 billion.[6] The value of OPIC's portfolio has ranged from about $11.2 billion to about $18 billion in fiscal years 2000 through 2014. OPIC officials stated that the agency's portfolio size is constrained by its administrative budget, as OPIC's ability to originate, develop, process, monitor, and execute transactions is directly related to its resources, primarily the number of staff its budget supports. In fiscal year 2015, OPIC employed approximately 230 full-time staff.

OPIC's Organizational Structure and Operations

OPIC's investment portfolio is managed by seven staff offices and departments, and the organization is overseen by an individual who serves as both President and Chief Executive Officer (CEO). Five offices and departments are responsible for managing OPIC's overall operations (see figure 2).

OPIC's Office of Investment Policy (OIP) is responsible for ensuring that all projects selected for funding comply with statutory requirements and general OPIC policy requirements, as well as for monitoring projects once they become active. According to OPIC officials, OIP works closely with OPIC's business lines to conduct a full policy review of all projects. In addition, the Department of Financial and Portfolio Management is responsible for the financial leadership and oversight of OPIC through financial management, controls, and risk and portfolio management.

In response to congressional committee reports encouraging OPIC to adopt an accountability mechanism, OPIC created the Office of Accountability in 2005. The office addresses concerns, complaints, or conflicts about OPIC activities. Project-affected communities, project sponsors, and project workers may approach the Office of Accountability to request that such concerns be reviewed and addressed. The office also provides mediation services. The director of the Office of Accountability is a senior level appointee approved by the OPIC President and CEO, and reports directly to the President and CEO.[7] According to OPIC officials, the director serves one 3-year term, may be reappointed for no more than one additional 3-year term, and may only be removed from office by a resolution of the Board of Directors.

OPIC Committed Over $20 Billion to Projects Worldwide for Fiscal Years 2008 through 2014

For fiscal years 2008 through 2014, OPIC committed approximately $20 billion in financing support to 718 projects worldwide (see figure 3).[8] As the figure illustrates, the average size of OPIC's commitments was higher from 2011 through 2014 compared with previous years, with the number of commitments declining while total commitment values were generally higher. This reflects, in part, OPIC's financing support for several large power generation and financial services projects during that period.

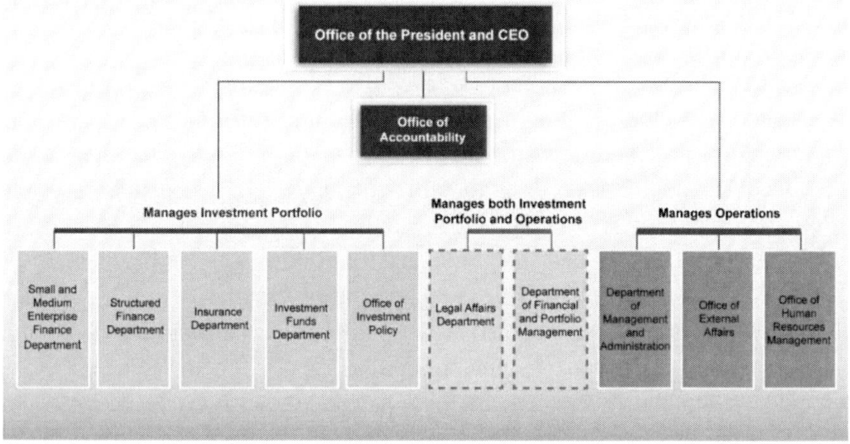

Source: OPIC. | GAO-16-64

Figure 2. Overseas Private Investment Corporation (OPIC) Organizational Structure Chart.

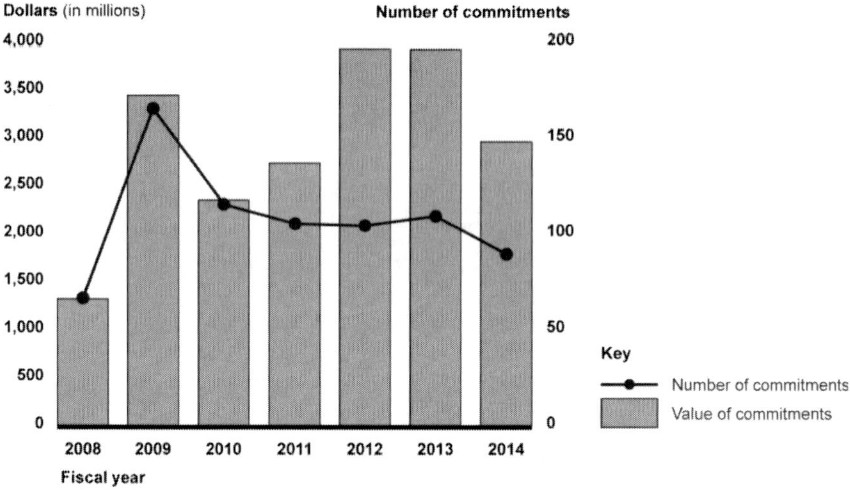

Source: GAO analysis of OPIC data. | GAO-16-64

Note: OPIC was not authorized to make new commitments for approximately half of fiscal year 2008, which may explain, in part, the significant difference between the total value of commitments in 2008 and 2009.

Figure 3. Overseas Private Investment Corporation's (OPIC) New Commitments Worldwide by Value and Number, Fiscal Years 2008 through 2014.

Financial Instruments

OPIC uses four financial instruments to support projects: loan guarantees, direct loans, investment funds, and political risk insurance.

- *Loan guarantees:* OPIC provides loan guarantees to third-party lenders. Loan guarantees provide a guarantee for loans underwritten by participating financial institutions according to agreed credit criteria and are typically provided in amounts up to $250 million.[9]
- *Direct loans:* OPIC provides direct loans to U.S. small businesses. The loans range from $600,000 to $50 million.
- *Investment funds:* OPIC facilitates equity investment in developing and emerging markets by providing debt financing to privately managed equity investment funds. These funds make direct equity and equity-related investments in portfolio companies, enabling U.S. firms to expand operations in overseas markets where they otherwise could not due to insufficient availability of resources.
- *Political risk insurance:* OPIC provides political risk insurance to cover certain political risks involved in investing in developing countries. According to OPIC officials, the share of insurance in OPIC's active portfolio has declined over the past 20 years due, in part, to the increasing number of private and public providers of political risk insurance.

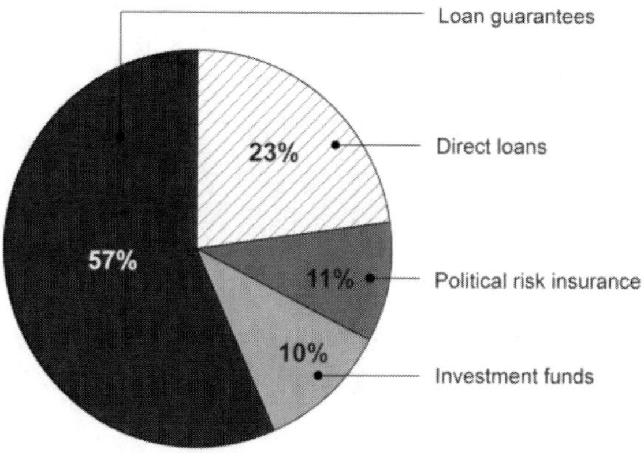

Source: GAO analysis of OPIC data. | GAO-16-64

Figure 4. Composition of Overseas Private Investment Corporation's (OPIC) New Commitments Worldwide by Financial Instrument Type, Fiscal Years 2008-2014.

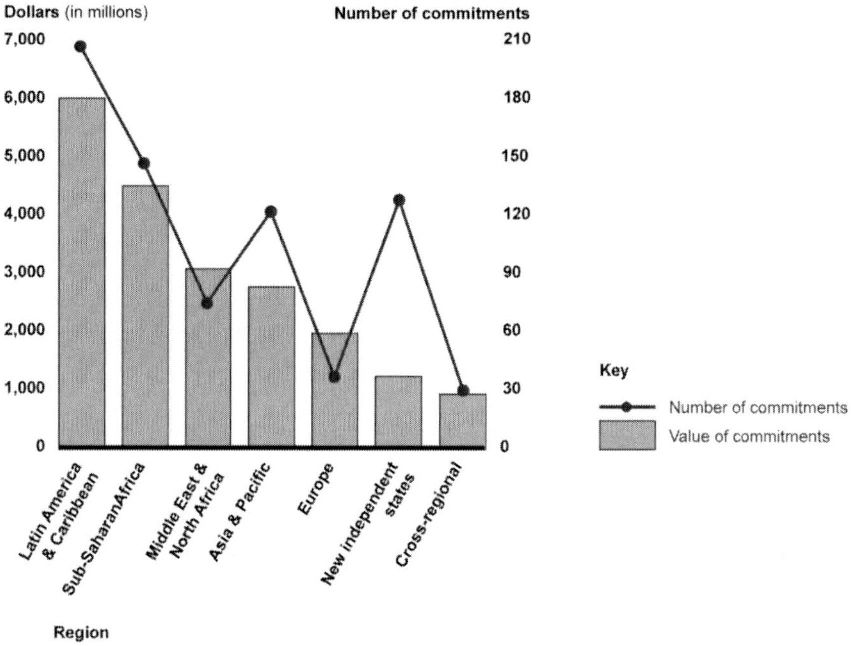

Source: GAO analysis of OPIC data. | GAO-16-64

Figure 5. Composition of Overseas Private Investment Corporation's (OPIC) New Commitments by Region, Fiscal Years 2008-2014.

In terms of value, the largest share of OPIC's new commitments worldwide in fiscal years 2008 through 2014 were loan guarantees, representing 57 percent of the approximately $20 billion total value of commitments made during the period (see figure 4).

Regions

During fiscal years 2008 through 2014, OPIC committed to projects in seven regional categories: Sub-Saharan Africa, Asia and the Pacific, Europe, Latin America and the Caribbean, the Middle East and Northern Africa, and New Independent States,[10] as well as investments designated for projects encompassing multiple countries and regions (cross- regional).[11] Figure 5 shows commitment values and numbers by region. In fiscal years 2008 through 2014, OPIC committed the majority of its new financing support to projects in two regions: Latin America and the Caribbean and Sub-Saharan

Africa. For example, OPIC is participating in the Power Africa initiative, which aims to support energy projects in Sub- Saharan Africa. In 2013, OPIC pledged to provide $1.5 billion for energy projects in Africa by 2018 and as of September 25, 2015, OPIC had already committed approximately $1.3 billion for Power Africa projects.

Country Income Levels

OPIC is required by law to give preferential consideration to investment projects in less developed countries that have per capita incomes of $984 or less in 1986 U.S. dollars, and restrict its activities in higher income countries with per capita incomes of $4,269 or more in 1986 U.S. dollars.[12] Based on these statutory definitions, OPIC categorizes countries' per capita incomes as low, middle, and high. The per capita income categories equate to the following in 2014 dollars: per capita incomes not greater than $1,836 for low income countries; between $1,836 and $7,964 for middle income countries; and greater than $7,964 for high income countries.[13] In fiscal years 2008 through 2014, OPIC's new commitments for projects in low per capita income countries represented 34 percent of the total number of new commitments and 25 percent of the total value. According to OPIC officials, based on legislative history, OPIC interprets the statutory requirement as allowing it to support projects in higher income countries that are highly developmental, focus on underserved areas or populations, or support U.S. small businesses.[14] See figure 6 for the composition of OPIC's fiscal years 2008 through 2014 commitments according to country per capita income level.[15]

Sectors

In fiscal years 2008 through 2014, OPIC committed the majority of its total new financing support to projects in the financial services sector—over half by value—and power generation sector[16]—almost one quarter by value (see figure 7). However, the majority of financing support OPIC provides to the financial services sector, primarily banks, is then lent to others for specified purposes, such as the lending to microfinance institutions or companies in other sectors. Nonfinancial services[17] and manufacturing are other key sectors OPIC supported, followed by agriculture, communications, construction, oil and gas, mining, tourism and hotels, and transportation. OPIC increased its commitments in power generation projects from about $1.4 million in fiscal year 2008 to approximately $1.2 billion in fiscal year 2014. Approximately 82 percent of OPIC's power generation commitments in fiscal years 2008 through 2014 were for renewable energy projects, reflecting OPIC's strategic focus on promoting renewable energy options in the developing world.

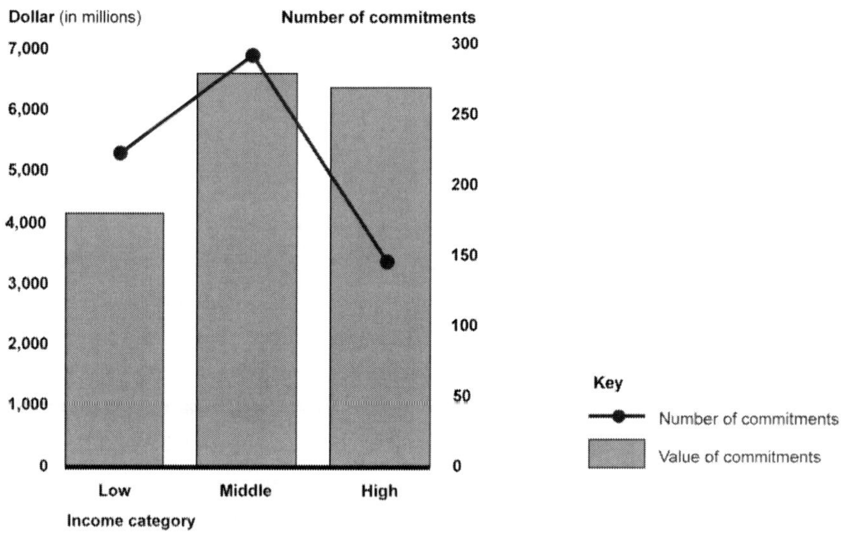

Source: GAO analysis of OPIC data. | GAO-16-64

Notes: For this analysis, we calculated the thresholds for the three per capita income categories for each fiscal year from 2008 through 2014 and categorized each commitment as low, middle, or high based on the World Bank's gross national income per capita for the project's host country in the year OPIC made the commitment. In 2014 dollars, the dollar thresholds for these categories were as follows: not greater than $1,836 for low income countries, between $1,836 and $7,964 for middle income countries, and greater than $7,964 for high income countries.

This analysis only includes OPIC projects located in a specific country. Seventy-four region-wide or cross-regional projects are excluded, which represents approximately $3.52 billion of the more than $20 billion committed during this period.

Figure 6. Composition of Overseas Private Investment Corporation's (OPIC) New Commitments by Country Per Capita Income Category, Fiscal Years 2008 through 2014.

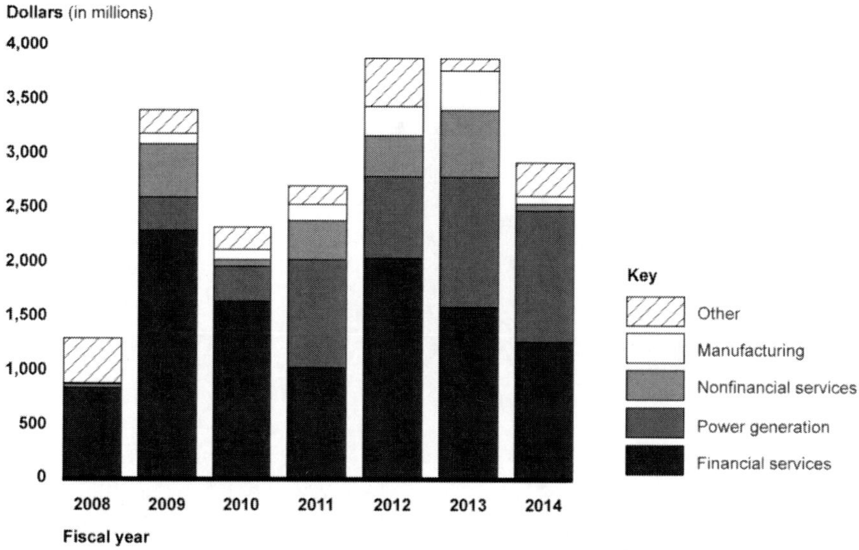

Source: GAO analysis of OPIC data. | GAO-16-64

Notes: The "Other" category includes the following sectors: agriculture, communications, construction, mining, oil and gas, tourism and hotels, and transportation. As measured by dollar value, approximately 82 percent of OPIC's power generation commitments in fiscal years 2008 through 2014 were for renewable energy projects.

Figure 7. Sector Trends in Overseas Private Investment Corporation's (OPIC) New Commitments Worldwide by Dollar Value, Fiscal Years 2008 through 2014.

OPIC's Commitments in Selected Countries Differed in Size and Industry Focus

OPIC commitments during fiscal years 2008 through 2014 varied for the four focus countries in our review—Honduras, Kenya, Pakistan, and Peru (see app. II for a list of all OPIC commitments made in the four countries during that period and app. III for brief descriptions of each of the 21 projects we selected for this review).[18] Of the four countries, Pakistan and Peru received the largest amount of new OPIC commitments with $646 million for 17 projects in Pakistan, and $625 million for 18 projects in Peru. New commitments in Honduras totaled $246 million for 11 projects, and in Kenya totaled $399 million for 11 projects. Kenya, Pakistan, and Peru each had OPIC investments in large-scale energy projects (see figure 8).

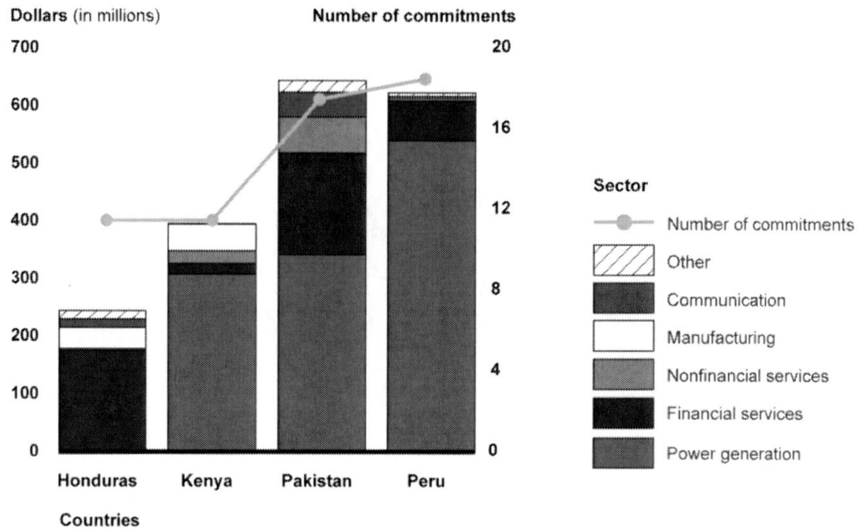

Source: GAO analysis of OPIC data. | GAO-16-64

Note: The "Other" category includes agriculture, construction, mining, oil and gas, tourism and hotels, and transportation.

Figure 8. Overseas Private Investment Corporation's (OPIC) New Commitments by Sector in Selected Countries, Fiscal Years 2008 through 2014.

OPIC Policies Guide Project Selection, and OPIC Recently Adopted Additional Guidance to Enhance the Policy Clearance Process

OPIC's Policies Guide the Project Selection Process

OPIC has established policies that guide its project selection process, which includes a review of projects' eligibility against OPIC policy and statutory requirements and due diligence reviews, among other evaluations. The process OPIC follows when reviewing potential projects is generally the same, with some modifications for projects that are supported through framework agreements between OPIC and large financial institutions.[19] This process has seven steps:

- Prescreening—informal review of proposals or discussions with potential applicants.
- Application intake—formal acceptance of application materials.
- Screening—initial review of a project against eligibility, financial, and legal requirements.
- Credit and legal due diligence reviews—formal evaluation of the risks to which a project may expose OPIC.
- Policy clearances—review of a project's impact on the U.S. economy, development in the host country, environmental and social issues, worker rights, and human rights.
- Final commitment review and approval—final approvals based on the project's level of financial risk.
- First disbursement—release of committed funds once an agreement is finalized.

A small percentage of project proposals and applications ultimately obtain financing support. According to OPIC, during fiscal years 2000 through 2012, officials prescreened about 20,000 project proposals and formally accepted 3,175 applications. About 37 percent of the 3,175 applications completed the full review process and reached disbursement (see figure 9), which is about 6 percent of the approximately 20,000 project proposals reviewed.

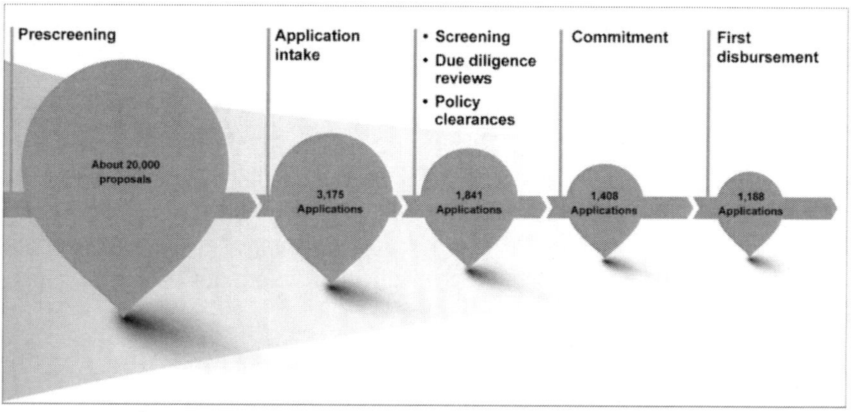

Source: OPIC. | GAO-16-64

Figure 9. Overseas Private Investment Corporation (OPIC) Application Review Pipeline and Project Selection Steps, Fiscal Years 2000 through 2012.

OPIC May Informally Prescreen Potential Applicants It Identifies Prior to Accepting an Application

Prior to formally accepting an application, OPIC staff may prescreen projects that they identify through several means. According to OPIC officials, OPIC relies on clients and partners, interagency contacts, and business development efforts to identify potential opportunities. For example, OPIC identifies opportunities through repeat clients, referrals, and large partner banks. OPIC also collaborates with several U.S. agencies to identify projects. For example, it is coordinating with State and the Trade Development Agency on the U.S.-Africa Clean Energy Finance Initiative, a 4-year, $15 million program to stimulate private sector investment in the African clean energy sector. In addition, embassy officials in Honduras and Pakistan said they try to identify potential projects for OPIC that support the embassy's strategic goals. Further, OPIC officials organize or participate in activities—such as workshops, conferences, and trade shows—to educate potential clients about OPIC. For example, OPIC organizes workshops, called Expanding Horizons, in several major cities each year.

OPIC staff prescreen projects through informal discussions with potential applicants by phone, email, and at events. This includes informally reviewing projects against OPIC's eligibility, financial, and policy requirements (discussed below). Applicants that successfully meet these requirements may formally submit their application and other required documents.

OPIC Screens Projects for Eligibility and Other Requirements

OPIC policy requires officials to screen accepted applications to identify flaws that may prevent an applicant's ultimate selection. This screening includes, among other things, the review of projects against OPIC policy and statutory requirements concerning eligibility restrictions and an initial review of the project's additionality—whether OPIC's support of a project "adds value" because it is a project that a private lender would not otherwise support given country risk or other factors.[20]

Connection to the United States

OPIC policy requires that there be a meaningful connection between an OPIC-supported project and the U.S. private sector. OPIC's guidance concerning the U.S. connection requirement outlines which entities are considered to be U.S. private sector entities and what constitutes sufficient

U.S. involvement. The U.S. connection requirement can be met by the applicant, the project company, or some other supporting entity, such as a services provider. Projects must meet both aspects of the U.S. connections policy requirement to obtain OPIC financing support, unless the President and CEO of OPIC approves a waiver or exception.

Table 1. U.S. Connection Requirements and Criteria for Overseas Private Investment Corporation (OPIC) Financing Support

Eligibility requirement	Criteria for meeting the requirement
U.S. entity	• OPIC considers the following to be U.S. private sector entities: an individual who is a U.S. citizen or lawful permanent resident of the U.S.; • a U.S. organized for-profit entity that is 25 percent or more U.S. owned; • a foreign organized for-profit entity that is majority (i.e., more than 50 percent) U.S. owned; • a U.S. organized nonprofit entity, regardless of the nationalities of its governing body members; or • a foreign organized nonprofit entity that is majority U.S. governed.
Type and extent of U.S. involvement	• OPIC may support a project when there is U.S. involvement in the project with a value that is equivalent to at least 25 percent of the project company's equity, which may be satisfied through one or more of the following: • equity investment; • long-term debt and guarantees; • grants; or • other contracts, including, but not limited to, construction, operating, maintenance or service, offtake purchase and supply contracts, surety bonds, and casualty insurance. • OPIC may support sub-loans through a framework agreement where OPIC guarantees a portion of loans made by the framework agreement partner (a financial intermediary) when the partner takes on a minimum of 25 percent of the risk of loss for the loan.

Source: OPIC. | GAO-16-64

OPIC's policies allow for substantial flexibility in implementing the U.S. connection requirement. For example, the U.S. connections requirement specifies that various entities can qualify as U.S. private sector entities, including a U.S. citizen or a nonprofit organized in the United States that may or may not have a U.S. board member.[21] Similarly, the requirement can be met through a U.S. entity's direct equity investment of at least 25 percent in the project or through subcontracting with a U.S. company for services, such as maintenance services, that equate to at least 25 percent of the project equity. Table 1 outlines OPIC's current criteria with respect to determining U.S. connections.

The 21 OPIC-sponsored projects we reviewed met the U.S. connection definition of an eligible U.S. entity in a number of ways.[22] Two projects were sponsored by a U.S. citizen; 12 were sponsored by a U.S. for-profit entity; 4 were sponsored by a U.S. nonprofit, 1 of which did not have any U.S. board members; and 3 met more than one of the criteria.

Applicants also met the U.S. involvement requirement in a number of ways. For example, for a school building project in Kenya the applicant provided over 25 percent of the equity for the project. In another case, a wind power project in Pakistan met the requirement by contracting with a large U.S. company to purchase wind turbine generators and operation and maintenance services worth more than 25 percent of the equity in the project. One OPIC client told us that he thought the U.S. sponsor needed to fund 25 percent of the project equity to obtain OPIC support. He later learned that similar projects in that country successfully met this requirement by contracting with or purchasing equipment from large U.S. companies, which he said was an easier way for project companies to meet OPIC's U.S. connection requirement. According to OPIC officials, OPIC may determine that a project company should meet specific criteria for the eligibility requirements due to credit-related factors.

Small Business Requirement for Direct Loans

OPIC's governing statute restricts the types of projects eligible for direct loans, and all the direct loan projects we reviewed met OPIC's small business requirement. OPIC can only provide direct loans to projects sponsored by or significantly involving U.S. small businesses or cooperatives.[23] OPIC defines small businesses as any business with annual revenues of less than $400 million in the last fiscal year, 500 or fewer employees, or any newly formed entity or individual owner that has a net worth of less than $100 million.[24]

Eight of the 21 projects we reviewed received a direct loan from OPIC, and all of these projects met OPIC's small business requirement.

Additionality

Screening also includes an initial review of the project's additionality.[25] Additionality in the OPIC context refers to whether or not OPIC's support of a project "adds value" because it is a project that a private lender would not otherwise support given country risk or other factors. We found that OPIC documented how all the projects in our sample met the additionality requirement. For example, 18 of the 21 projects met the additionality requirement because the host country had high country risk ratings (see table 2).

Table 2. How Selected Overseas Private Investment Corporation (OPIC) Projects Met Additionality Requirements

Number of projects[a]	Additionality qualification	Example projects
18	Country risk	A project in Honduras was rated as high risk through the Interagency Country Risk Assessment System, an interagency process through which the credit risk associated with U.S. credit assistance to foreign countries is assessed periodically.
6	Length of the loan period	A framework partner was able to provide a longer term loan to a microfinance bank in Pakistan than it could have obtained on the local market because OPIC provided a loan guarantee.
6	Project innovation	A project in Honduras planned to introduce a new production process in the host country.
4	Lack of private sector funding	For a solar power project in Peru, no commercial banks were willing to provide financing without a loan guarantee.
4	Benefits to the area	Three of the projects provided benefits to an underdeveloped sector in the host country.
3	Project size	A geothermal power project in Kenya needed a $310 million loan guarantee.

Source: GAO analysis of OPIC project documentation. | GAO-16-64

[a] Projects may have met the additionality requirement in more than one way.

U.S. embassy officials and OPIC clients we met with in Honduras and Pakistan stressed that high levels of country risk severely inhibited private sector financing. For example, one client noted that it was not willing to assume the risk of financing a project in Honduras without a loan guarantee from OPIC or another development finance institution. In addition, two OPIC clients in Pakistan said that local banks offer shorter term loans and one client noted that other development finance institutions offered financing options at high interest rates that were unreasonable for nonprofit organizations. Lastly, three OPIC clients we interviewed in Honduras and Pakistan said that they could not fund their project without OPIC due to a lack of private sector funding.

Completion of Screening

Based on the completed screening, OPIC either rejects the project, suggests changes to the applicant to improve the likelihood of acceptance, or moves the project forward. For projects deemed ready to advance, an OPIC official concurrently initiates credit and legal due diligence reviews and the policy clearance process.

OPIC Conducts Credit and Legal due Diligence Reviews

OPIC conducts credit and legal due diligence reviews to identify and evaluate risks to which OPIC may be exposed. According to OPIC policy, the credit due diligence review includes, in part, evaluation of the financial condition of key project participants; markets and marketing strategy; project management quality and structure; financial projections; project country political and economic analysis; and credit checks for key project participants.[26] OPIC policy states that the legal due diligence review consists of legal and regulatory evaluations concerning, for example, the complexity of the legal framework in the host country and the jurisdiction of the governing law for various project agreements. OPIC is also to conduct character risk due diligence on the project company, the borrower, and other relevant entities in accordance with OPIC policy, to uncover any derogatory information about an OPIC project, its sponsors, investors, or key personnel to minimize risks to OPIC's portfolio and reputation.[27] Satisfactory completion of the character risk due diligence is a non-waivable condition of any binding OPIC commitment. When issues of concern are identified, OPIC staff are required to provide a detailed analysis of such issues and related recommendations to upper management and, potentially, the President and CEO of OPIC.

Based on our review of project file documentation, we found that OPIC conducted credit and character risk due diligence reviews when required.[28] For example, for one project we reviewed, OPIC identified a potential character risk due diligence issue concerning one of the project's contractors. OPIC staff conducted additional due diligence reviews related to these issues, appropriately documented the concerns and resolution, and alerted management to the potential issue.[29]

OPIC Requires the Completion of Four Policy Clearances for Each Project

OPIC policy requires officials to document the completion of four distinct policy clearances for each project: (1) U.S. economic effect and host- country developmental impact, (2) environmental and social impacts, (3) worker rights, and (4) human rights. OIP officials are to conduct these reviews, based on applications, responses to questionnaires, other client- provided documentation, and other information. We found that OIP completed the four policy clearances for all 21 projects in our sample. In addition, according to OIP officials, they participate in screening discussions and attend other credit-related project meetings to learn more about the financial structure of the potential project and to share any potential policy-related risks with other OPIC officials. The specific review processes are outlined in OPIC policies, which have evolved over time.[30] Figure 10 outlines the policy clearance structure.

Policy clearances	Economic impacts		Environmental and social impacts	Worker rights	Human rights
	U.S. economic effect	Host country development impact			
Guiding OPIC policies	• Procedural Guidelines for U.S. Economic Impact Analysis • Procedures for Conducting Performance Requirement Analysis	• Expanded Development Impact Profile Guidelines • Financial Services Development Impact Profile Guidelines	• Environmental and Social Policy Statement • Office of Investment Policy Procedures Manual		
OPIC group responsible for clearance	Office of Investment Policy – Economic Impact Analysis Group		Office of Investment Policy – Environmental and Social Group	Office of Investment Policy – Labor and Human Rights Group	

Source: GAO analysis of OPIC documents. | GAO-16-94

Figure 10. Overseas Private Investment Corporation (OPIC) Policy Clearances, Guiding Policies, and Responsible OPIC Groups.

U.S. Economic and Host Country Development Clearance

This clearance has two distinct reviews—the project's expected impact on the U.S. economy and on development in the host country.

- **U.S. economic impact.** Congress directed OPIC to seek to support projects that have positive trade benefits for the United States and to decline projects expected to cause any significant reduction in U.S employment if the reduction is occurring because the investment involves substantially the same product for the same market.[31] OPIC has guidelines for conducting U.S. economic impact analysis, and relies largely on applicant-provided project information. In some cases, OPIC policy requires the development of an industry analysis to assess the health of the U.S. industry to determine whether the project's output could potentially harm U.S. jobs.
- **Host-country development impacts.** OPIC is required by law to prepare and maintain statistics on each project's impact on development in the host country, and to report its assessment of the development impact to Congress each year.[32] According to OPIC officials, OPIC conducted qualitative assessments of each project's expected development impact prior to 2000. OPIC also collected and reported on quantitative information such as host-country job creation and tax payments. OPIC officials stated that they sought to make the estimated development impact more quantifiable with the creation of its Development Impact Matrix, which uses both qualitative and quantitative measures to establish a development impact score that enables comparison across projects. The matrix includes specific indicators for physical investments and financial services projects. This matrix has been updated twice since 2007, and according to officials the updates have been based on site visits, feedback from USAID, and best practices, and OPIC is currently in the process of updating it for a third time (see app. IV for an example of OPIC's development impact scoring).

OPIC reports each year on the estimated development impact of new projects committed in that year in its Annual Report on Development Impact, in accordance with statutory requirements. For example, in its 2013 report, OPIC estimated that new projects committed in fiscal year 2013 would result in $8.9 billion in investments in developing and emerging markets and create almost 18,000 jobs in host countries.[33] According to officials, OPIC determines the estimated development impact by evaluating estimates provided by the client and scoring the relevant indicators for a project during the policy clearance process.

However, estimating meaningful information on development impacts is inherently difficult. Officials from OPIC and IFC—the World Bank's development finance institution—stated that demonstration effects and spillover effects of projects can be critical to development but are difficult to identify and measure. For example, IFC officials said that it is difficult to measure the ability of a successful new project to spur similar projects in a country.

INTERNATIONAL FINANCE CORPORATION (IFC) PERFORMANCE STANDARDS

The IFC standards address project risks related to the following eight standards:

1. Assessment and management of environmental and social risks and impacts.
2. Labor and working conditions.
3. Resource efficiency and pollution prevention.
4. Community health, safety, and security.
5. Land acquisition and involuntary resettlement.
6. Biodiversity conservation and resource sustainability.
7. Indigenous peoples.
8. Cultural heritage.

Source: IFC. | GAO-16-64

Environmental and Social Impacts, Worker Rights, and Human Rights Clearances

Congress directed OPIC to issue a comprehensive set of environmental, transparency, worker rights, and human rights guidelines that are binding on OPIC, consistently applied to all projects, and at least as rigorous as the environmental and social policies developed by the IFC in 2009.[34] According to officials, OPIC's Environmental and Social Policy Statement, effective in 2010, addresses this requirement. OPIC's Environmental and Social Policy Statement describes its standards and assessment and monitoring requirements for environmental and social, worker rights, and human rights impacts.[35] The statement also adopts the IFC's Performance Standards on Environmental and Social Sustainability.[36] According to OPIC officials, OPIC's OIP Procedures Manual guides officials' implementation of the Environmental and Social Policy Statement.

- **Environmental and social impacts clearance.** OPIC, as required by policy, categorizes projects as A, B, C, or D based on environmental and social risk factors, and this categorization determines the level of review and monitoring a project receives.[37] Further, OPIC is to consider direct, indirect, induced, regional, trans-boundary and cumulative environmental and social impacts when categorizing projects during the environmental and social clearance process. According to officials, OIP also reviews and documents human rights issues, such as community health and safety, land ownership, and indigenous peoples, as part of the environmental and social clearance process.

  Category A projects represent the highest risk for environmental and social impacts, with the categorization based on the inherent risk of the project before any mitigation measures are taken.[38] Category A projects represented 3 percent of OPIC's active projects as of June 30, 2015. OPIC's Environmental and Social Policy Statement provides qualitative definitions for the four environmental and social categories, and it includes a list of sensitive sectors and project factors that may lead to a Category A categorization.

  OPIC's Environmental and Social Policy Statement and OPIC's governing statute requires that Category A projects undergo additional review during the selection and monitoring phases, including

  - review of an applicant-provided environmental and social impact assessment, including a 60-day public comment period;[39]
  - additional post-selection monitoring, such as third-party audits; and
  - at least one monitoring site visit to each project within 3 years of finalizing the agreement, to the extent feasible.

  According to officials, OPIC has visited every Category A project as required, except for two projects that officials were unable to visit due to security concerns.

  OPIC's Environmental and Social Policy Statement also specifies categorical prohibitions, which are projects that OPIC will not fund.

For example, OPIC will not fund the construction of certain large dams.[40]

- **Worker rights clearance.** In accordance with its governing legislation, OPIC will only support projects in countries that have, or are taking steps to adopt, laws that uphold internationally recognized worker rights.[41] The Environmental and Social Policy Statement includes guidance for determining if a country meets labor eligibility requirements. OPIC considers as eligible any country on the Generalized System of Preferences list,[42] because that status indicates they meet certain internationally recognized worker rights.[43] According to officials, OIP also reviews and documents human rights issues that specifically concern labor rights, such as forced and child labor issues, as part of the worker rights clearance process.

  In 2010, OPIC introduced the Special Consideration classification for projects with a higher risk of violating labor rights. OPIC may classify projects as Special Consideration based on an assessment of the likelihood, severity, and degree of possible labor rights violations, and their relevance to a project. OPIC has designated 10 projects as Special Consideration since that time.[44] OPIC requires all Special Consideration projects to submit an annual labor report summarizing workplace conditions and to conduct one third-party audit within the first 3 years of operations. In addition, OPIC policy states that it will endeavor to conduct at least one OPIC site visit within 3 years of the execution of the OPIC agreement.
- **Human rights clearance.** OPIC's governing legislation directs it to consult with the Secretary of State and take into account all available information concerning the effect of a project on human rights and fundamental freedoms in the host country.[45] OPIC's policies require that it screen projects using a process mutually agreed upon by OPIC and State, which State documented in a 2006 memorandum. The memorandum designates which agency is responsible for providing human rights reviews, depending on the current status of human rights violations in a country and project characteristics such as sector and degree of host government involvement. This status is documented in the human rights sensitivity list maintained by OPIC and reviewed quarterly by State. The list includes all the countries in which OPIC is authorized to conduct activities and is divided into three categories based on the human rights situation in each country. The

responsibility for conducting the review is based on the project country categorization and other information.[46]

OPIC documents when a human rights clearance has been conducted for each project, regardless of which agency provides the clearance. OPIC officials said that the purpose of this human rights clearance document is only to confirm that a clearance occurred, in accordance with the statutory requirement to consult with State on the effect of a project on human rights in the host country.

According to OPIC officials, when OPIC conducts the human rights review, it bases the clearance approval on a review of human rights issues and the documentation of that review in other clearance documents. As discussed above, OPIC conducts the review and documentation of relevant human rights issues during the environmental and social and worker rights clearance processes, according to OPIC officials.[47] In reviewing the clearances for 21 projects, we identified 2 projects for which OPIC did not document its review of human rights issues in the environmental and social clearance or the worker rights clearance. However, the clearances for these two projects did include human rights-related conditions that the project companies would need to meet to obtain OPIC financing support. In addition, OPIC completed the clearances for these two projects in 2006 and 2007, which, according to OPIC officials, predate newer policies concerning policy clearance documentation.[48]

Approval for Commitment and First Disbursement Is Based on Project's Level of Financial Risk

After completion of the credit and legal due diligence reviews and the four policy clearances, OPIC management reviews projects based on the financial level of risk each project poses, with the largest projects—those valued at more than $50 million—requiring approval from OPIC's Board of Directors.[49] OPIC's board reviewed and approved sixteen percent of the number of commitments OPIC made in fiscal years 2008 through 2014, which constitutes 72 percent of the total dollar value of these commitments. Thirteen percent of the number of commitments OPIC made during this period—representing 67 percent of the total dollar value—were for amounts greater than $50 million. Several commitments were approved by the board for reasons other than monetary value.[50]

For commitments requiring board approval, OPIC is to solicit input from its board members—eight members from the private sector and seven from the federal government, including OPIC, the Departments of Commerce, Labor, State, Treasury, USAID, and USTR. Prior to board meetings, OPIC provides board members with key project documents. According to officials from OPIC, State, Treasury, USAID, and USTR, it is routine for board members to discuss specific issues regarding the projects among themselves and with OPIC prior to the meetings. For example, USTR officials stated that USTR provides guidance and oversight on project selection concerning a proposed project's impact on U.S. trade policy. According to State officials, the agency provides guidance with respect to foreign policy considerations, such as whether OPIC should support projects in a particular country because of current political considerations, or the reputations of sponsors and investors. A State official said that they generally raise concerns with OPIC earlier in the vetting process, but occasionally contentious issues arise for projects presented for board approval. These issues have in some cases been resolved through the inclusion of mitigation measures such as conditions to the loan agreements.

A project reaches commitment when it receives final management approval and a legally binding document is signed. At commitment, OPIC creates the budgetary or financial obligation for the project. As shown in figure 9 above, about 16 percent of applications that reached commitment during the fiscal year 2000 through 2012 period did not reach disbursement. According to OPIC officials, OPIC may, for example, be unable to reach a final agreement with the client concerning loan terms. After the initial disbursement, OPIC's monitoring functions assume responsibility for the projects in accordance with OPIC policy.

OPIC Recently Developed Additional Guidance for Conducting Human Rights Reviews

OPIC recently developed additional guidance to identify responsibilities concerning the review of specific human rights issues and enhance human rights due diligence procedures. Although OPIC had established policies for the project selection process, we found during the course of our work that these policies did not provide comprehensive guidance for reviewing and documenting human rights information that is required to be considered for assistance. OPIC officials said that the review of human rights issues is done as part of its environmental and social and worker rights clearances, consistent with the IFC Performance Standards. However, we found that neither OPIC's Environmental and Social Policy Statement nor the OIP *Procedures Manual* provided comprehensive guidance on the human rights issues that OPIC officials should consider during the clearance process, or how these reviews should be carried out and documented.

We further found that OPIC's policies did not clearly identify the requirements and delineate responsibilities for considering human rights information. OPIC's Environmental and Social Policy Statement requires all projects to meet applicable IFC Performance Standards. The IFC Performance Standards do not explicitly address human rights but, rather, the standards state that human rights issues are addressed throughout the standards. Although OPIC's policies require the Environmental and Social Group and the Labor and Human Rights Group to identify those IFC Performance Standards relevant to their review of a project in the clearance document, the policies did not dictate which performance standards each team is responsible for addressing.

When we discussed our concerns with OPIC officials, they agreed that the documentation of their human rights reviews was not clear. In response, OPIC developed additional guidance establishing roles and responsibilities for human rights reviews. This new guidance outlines how specific human rights issues covered in the Universal Declaration of Human Rights correspond to the IFC Performance Standards and assigns responsibility within OIP for reviewing and documenting each issue.

OPIC has also taken steps to strengthen its human rights reviews in response to a 2014 report by its Office of Accountability, which recommended that OPIC establish enhanced human rights due diligence procedures.[51] In February 2014, OPIC's senior management requested the Office of Accountability to conduct an independent review of OPIC's experience with two related projects in Liberia for which they received a number of complaints. In 2008, OPIC approved the two projects, a biofuel project and a 35-megawatt power plant project owned by the same parent company. The report found that OPIC's human rights policies did not state when enhanced human rights due diligence should be triggered during project selection.

In a March 2015 congressionally mandated response to the Office of Accountability's report,[52] OPIC reported that it had, among other things, (1) developed enhanced screening procedures to better identify factors contributing to higher human rights related risks and (2) deployed specialized social consultants to project sites as part of the human rights due diligence review. OPIC is currently following draft guidance for enhanced screening procedures developed in response to the Office of Accountability recommendation. Under these procedures, projects with heightened risk may be required to undergo additional third party audits based on the draft guidance. However, the draft guidance does not describe who is responsible for conducting this review or how it is to be documented. According to officials, OPIC identified five new projects as higher risk in 2015 and will require these projects to participate in third party audits once the projects are operational. OPIC also hired three specialized social consultants, and has identified a number of additional social consultants with whom the agency can contract with when necessary. According to OPIC officials, the agency plans to finalize the draft screening procedures for the enhanced human rights due diligence reviews in coordination with its update of the Environmental and Social Policy Statement and OIP Procedures Manual.[53]

OPIC Recently Adopted Additional Guidelines for Conducting Cumulative Impact Assessments

OPIC recently adopted additional guidelines for conducting cumulative impact assessments that may support more systematic analyses. According to OPIC policy, OPIC is to categorize projects based, in part, on its preliminary assessment of the potential environmental and social risks and impacts—including cumulative impacts—of a project in the absence of any required mitigation. Cumulative impacts are those that result from the successive, incremental, or combined effects of an action, project, or activity in combination with other existing, planned, or reasonably anticipated future projects or activities. Cumulative impact assessments are conducted to analyze the potential impacts and risks that proposed projects and activities—including projects supported by other organizations or companies—will have on valued environmental and social components, such as biodiversity, water supply, and cultural heritage. Cumulative impact assessments can be challenging to conduct, because cumulative impacts can depend on factors for which complete information, such as details of other companies' project designs, is not available or is difficult to obtain. According to the IFC's 2013 handbook for conducting cumulative impact assessments, a comprehensive assessment requires the participation of many parties and is best led by local governments or regional planners because effectively designing and implementing the assessment is often beyond the capacity of a single developer.

OPIC committed to supporting four wind power projects in one region in Pakistan before the completion of an OPIC-contracted cumulative impact assessment. However, OPIC officials told us that they approved the projects because available evidence indicated that the wind power projects would not cause significant cumulative impacts. In the environmental and social clearances for the two wind power projects in Pakistan we reviewed,[54] OPIC noted that there were 14 proposed wind power projects in the region and that each planned to produce 50 megawatts of energy.[55] The clearances stated that as a result, there is the potential for cumulative impacts to the community, biodiversity, and resource availability. Although the United Nations Development Program commissioned a regional environmental assessment of the region in 2009 that considered cumulative impacts, the analysis was qualitative and only provided general guidelines for future studies. OPIC stated in its environmental and social clearances for the two projects we reviewed that it would hire an independent consultant to conduct a cumulative impact analysis. However, OPIC committed to these two wind power projects in 2013 and another two in the same region in 2014 before the completion of the OPIC-contracted cumulative impact assessment.[56]

According to OPIC officials, they approved the four wind power projects because they did not believe that the projects would result in significant cumulative impacts. OPIC officials told us that the three cumulative impact issues typically associated with wind power projects are threats to biodiversity, increased noise levels, and shadow flicker.[57] OPIC made a determination that the projects posed no significant impact to birds based on an analysis conducted by the World Wildlife Foundation. OPIC officials said that noise and shadow flicker could be more easily mitigated and, because the area is not heavily populated, potential noise and shadow flicker impacts would not impact a significant number of people. Based on this information, OPIC issued the final environmental and social clearances with conditions that were incorporated into the contracts for the four wind power projects.[58]

OPIC adopted the IFC handbook for conducting cumulative impact assessments and plans to provide the guidelines to potential clients. OPIC required the contractor that conducted the 2015 cumulative impact assessment of wind power projects in Pakistan to follow these guidelines when conducting the assessment. According to officials, they did not have adequate information from the government of Pakistan or other organizations about the design of other planned wind farms to conduct an analytical assessment of the potential impact on noise levels and shadow flicker until 2015. OPIC officials said they plan to provide clients with the IFC handbook to support their environmental and social assessments. However, OPIC officials noted that they will not be able to require clients to use the IFC handbook because it may be too difficult for clients to collect all the necessary information for conducting such a cumulative impact assessment.

OPIC MONITORS PROJECTS, BUT SITE VISIT REPORTS ARE NOT ALWAYS TIMELY, AND USE OF CLIENT-REPORTED DATA INVOLVES RISKS

OPIC Uses Several Tools to Monitor Policy Compliance and Development Impacts of Its Projects

OPIC is required to monitor ongoing projects' compliance with environmental, social, labor, and human rights requirements, and assesses U.S. economic impact and host-country development impact. OPIC uses several tools to monitor policy compliance and development impacts: (1) annual self-monitoring questionnaires (SMQs), (2) site visits by OPIC staff, and (3) other independent and client-provided reports, such as reports from independent engineers or third-party audits or project-specific environmental or labor reports. On the basis of our document review, we found that three sections of OIP—the Environmental and Social Group, the Labor and Human Rights Group, and the Economic Impact Analysis Group—participate in OPIC's integrated monitoring and assessment process in accordance with OPIC policy. The Environmental and Social Group and Labor and Human Rights Group conduct compliance monitoring while the Economic Impact Analysis Group assesses U.S. economic and host-country development impacts. According to OPIC policy, these groups may conduct site visits separately or concurrently. Other groups within OPIC are also required to monitor projects. For example, according to OPIC officials, its Department of Financial and Portfolio Management and Investment Funds Department monitor the financial performance of OPIC projects at least annually.[59]

Self-Monitoring Questionnaires

OPIC requires its clients to report annually on compliance with project requirements, as well as on U.S. economic and host-country development impact, by completing an online SMQ. The format of an SMQ is consistent across projects. According to OPIC officials, SMQs are a data gathering tool designed to provide OPIC with an annual snapshot of projects' operational performance on nonfinancial metrics, and to identify potential red flags for projects, such as non-compliance with local environmental or worker safety laws. SMQs provide project information such as total number of employees, whether the project has implemented initiatives directed at restoring or preserving the environment, and whether general work conditions comply with labor laws.

OPIC policy requires that clients submit an SMQ annually after the first full year of operations and that OPIC follow up with clients that do not submit SMQs in a timely manner. According to officials, SMQs are not required from clients who receive a site monitoring visit during the course of the fiscal year because that same information is gathered by OPIC on site. In 2014, OPIC received 348 SMQs from 405 projects for which SMQs were required, a response rate of 86 percent. For fiscal years 2008 through 2014, the response rate ranged from 61 to 96 percent (see table 3). According to OPIC policy, clients who miss reporting deadlines receive a reminder from OIP, and in cases of no response, a communication from the Legal Affairs Department. OPIC officials stated that a missing SMQ may indicate that the client is experiencing financial or other difficulties and could trigger an OPIC site visit.[60]

Site Monitoring

Policy site monitoring is designed to provide OPIC with a comprehensive view of an active project's performance in terms of compliance with environmental, social, labor, and human rights requirements and the impacts on the U.S. economy and host-country development, according to OPIC officials. Each year, OIP visits a small percentage of active projects. In 2014, OIP made site monitoring visits to 51 out of 405 active projects, or about 13 percent. For fiscal years 2008 through 2014, OIP site visits as a percentage of active projects ranged from 9 to 13 percent (see table 4).[61] Because most OPIC projects are active for a number of years, the total percentage of projects visited by OIP is higher than the percentage of active projects receiving site visits in any one year.

Table 3. Overseas Private Investment Corporation's (OPIC) Self-Monitoring Questionnaire (SMQ) Response Rates, Fiscal Years 2008-2014

Year	2008	2009	2010	2011	2012	2013	2014
SMQs required	430	472	412	404	353	316	405
SMQs received	261	314	395	321	333	289	348
Percentage response rate	61%	67%	96%	79%	94%	91%	86%

Source: OPIC. | GAO-16-64

Table 4. Numbers and Percentages of Overseas Private Investment Corporation's (OPIC) Site Visits for Policy Monitoring, Fiscal Years 2008-2014

Year	2008	2009	2010	2011	2012	2013	2014
Total number of active projects	430	472	412	404	353	316	405
Total number of site visits	46	57	35	38	32	32	51
Site visits as a percentage of active projects	11%	12%	9%	9%	9%	10%	13%

Source: GAO calculations based on OPIC data. | GAO-16-64

Note: In the table, the number of required self-monitoring questionnaires (SMQs) is used as a proxy for the number of total active projects each year. Active projects include some projects that are not yet operational.

In accordance with OPIC policy, OPIC uses a combination of risk-based and random sampling to select projects for site visits, although OPIC officials told us that cost effectiveness and travel logistics also play a role in site selection. For example, for environmental and social compliance monitoring, Category A projects receive the highest priority for site visit monitoring; for labor compliance monitoring, projects classified as Special Consideration receive highest priority. According to our analysis of OPIC data, random sampling accounted for about half of the 291 total site visits conducted by OIP for fiscal years 2008 through 2014, on average. This percentage varied each year and ranged from 22 percent in 2014 to 84 percent in 2011.

According to OPIC officials, OPIC asks clients to complete a project information report prior to site visits.[62] The report is similar to an SMQ, but also incorporates information provided in the project's original application. For example, the project information report asks for a description of any corrective measures taken on any occupational health and safety or environmental issues emerging from OPIC's reviews, and descriptions of government decrees, laws, directives, or agreements that affect project imports and exports—information that is not included in SMQs. The report requests revised estimates, through the fifth year of project operations, for total remittances, employment levels, and project sales—information similar to that requested in SMQs.

OPIC conducted site visits for 3 of the 21 projects in our sample,[63] and in our review of the site visit reports, we found that OPIC identified a lack of compliance with project requirements at each of the 3 project sites. For example, a monitoring site visit to a project in Honduras revealed that not all personnel were wearing appropriate protective equipment and that construction materials were inappropriately discarded or stored on site, information that was not provided by the client in the SMQs. In addition, OPIC officials stated that they prioritized a site visit in 2011 to a palm oil production facility in Honduras that was a Category B project because the industry is considered sensitive due to its potential environmental and social impacts.[64] According to the site visit report, OPIC officials found that several conditions specified in the loan agreement had not been met, and they provided a list of follow-up actions that the company agreed to take, including suspension of the use of a specific pesticide and corrective actions concerning the company's fuel consumption and estimate of greenhouse gases. Following the visit, OPIC requested and received additional documentation from the client to verify that it had addressed the 2011 site visit recommendations.

Site monitoring is also used to verify and reassess a project's impact on the U.S. economy and on host-country development. OPIC officials told us that this impact reassessment would ideally take place 5 years after a project becomes operational, but because of resource constraints, trips are sometimes combined and reassessments take place earlier.[65] For the 3 site visit reports we reviewed, we found that OPIC visited 1 project 10 months after final disbursement of funds, another project about 2 years after it became operational, and the third a little over 3 years after it became operational. During site visits, OPIC officials rescore the development indicators to determine the extent to which the client is meeting the development goals outlined in its application. Thus, the initial estimate of the "number of persons employed at the fifth year of operations" is compared to the actual number of persons employed by the project at the time of the visit, and the jobs indicator is adjusted accordingly. For example, according to OPIC officials, after a site visit to a project in Honduras, the Economic Impact Analysis Group concluded that the project had a stronger impact on local job creation than initially expected, giving a higher score for that indicator. Overall, for the 3 projects we reviewed that received site visits, 2 received a lower overall development score once all indicators were reassessed, with 1 of the 2 changing classification from "highly developmental" to "developmental"; the third project received a higher overall score after the site visit.

Site Visit Reports Were Not Always Prepared in a Timely Manner

OPIC did not document the results of the 3 project site visits in our sample in a timely manner, which may limit their usefulness. Two of the 3 site visit reports we reviewed were written several years after the site visits occurred. According to OPIC officials, staff who made the site visit orally present findings in internal meetings shortly after each visit. OPIC policy does not require that site visit reports be completed and submitted to management in a designated period of time. According to OPIC officials, OIP staff document and submit site visit monitoring reports when time permits. However, federal internal control standards dictate that agencies develop controls that ensure that actions are taken to address risk, such as the accurate and timely recording of events.[66] In addition to using site visits for project monitoring, OPIC uses information collected during site visits when reviewing similar projects for clearance to help predict potential development impacts and refine development indicators, according to OPIC officials. Thus, the lack of timely documentation of site visits may limit the value of this information for reviewing and estimating the impact of potential future projects. OPIC officials told us that they are in the process of creating a standardized process for documenting site visits, which they expect will make it faster for teams to complete trip reports.

OPIC May Not Have Adequate Information on Some Projects' Status

OPIC's use of client-reported data from SMQs, combined with limited site visits, may not provide OPIC adequate information on project's policy compliance and development impact status in some cases. OPIC is required by law to monitor and report on the economic and social development impacts of its projects.[67] Federal internal control standards call for management to obtain relevant and accurate data and to identify risks related to meeting defined objectives.[68] According to OPIC officials, OPIC reviews and uses data that are submitted by the client in SMQs for monitoring the majority of its projects on an annual basis; however, the data are not validated by OPIC's staff or an independent reviewer. OPIC officials noted that the client is responsible for ensuring that the data it provides in the SMQs are accurate and clients must attest to the accuracy of the data they provide. In our analysis of 21 OPIC projects from Honduras, Kenya, Pakistan, and Peru, clients for 14 of the projects were required to complete SMQs because the projects had been active and operational. Of these 14 projects, all but one of the clients submitted the required annual SMQ. In addition, clients for 11 of these 14 projects fully completed the SMQs they submitted. The clients for the remaining 3 projects left sections of the SMQs unanswered. Specifically, we found that one client did not report employment numbers; a second client did not report the date that a project became operational; and a third client did not report remittances and revenue amounts.

In fulfilling its requirement to report on social and economic development impacts, OPIC faces risks related to the accuracy of client-reported data because self-reported statements may not reflect actual project conditions. OPIC officials told us that limited staff resources constrain its ability to verify the accuracy of data in the SMQs and that they rely on a contractor to conduct a high-level review of SMQs to identify blank, incomplete, or obviously incorrect responses.

Further, because OIP officials only visit a small number of projects each year, OIP largely relies on the SMQs for updated annual information about some projects' compliance with project requirements. OPIC's 2013 Annual Report on Development Impact, submitted to Congress, omitted data for 34 out of 315 SMQs because, according to the report, the data did not meet the agency's data quality standards. Also, as previously discussed, we found several noncompliance issues in the site visit reports we reviewed, which clients had not identified or described in detail in the SMQs. During the 291 site visits conducted by OPIC in fiscal years 2008 through 2014, it identified 49 project sites with environmental and social noncompliance issues and 9 project sites with labor and human rights noncompliance issues. Of these, clients had reported noncompliance issues for only 18 projects in SMQs. Common issues identified by OPIC included late or missing required quarterly and annual reports, safety issues such as cluttered hallways, and missing documentation such as company human resource policies. However, more serious environmental and social risks were identified during a 2013 monitoring visit, where corrective actions for meeting environmental and social compliance requirements were needed that the client did not have sufficient resources to implement. As a result, OPIC terminated its support of the project.

A 2014 OPIC Office of Accountability Report stated that during the selection process, when the agency is considering whether to support a project that may have high development risks, OPIC should confirm that its staff capacity and other resources are sufficient for needed client engagement and monitoring.[69] In addition, the report found that OPIC needs "monitoring systems…which are proportionate to the risks that could adversely affect the achievement of desired development outcomes." In response to these findings, OPIC said it has taken steps to ensure that it has sufficient capacity and resources to review and monitor projects. Without analyzing the risk to information quality inherent in its project monitoring process, OPIC cannot be assured that risk from using client-reported data is within an appropriate risk tolerance to achieve OPIC's monitoring objectives.

According to officials, OPIC, in some cases, also uses independent and client-provided reports to verify some projects' compliance with policies. For example, according to OPIC officials, OPIC requires certain large projects to allow an independent engineer to conduct environmental compliance site visits on a quarterly or semi-annual basis. In addition, all Category A projects and those categorized as Special Consideration are required to undergo a third party audit within 3 years of becoming operational. Further, officials said OPIC includes a condition in some clients' contracts that requires them to provide annual reports concerning, for example, pollutant level measurements and worker safety information (e.g., number of accidents). Officials stated that these reports provide additional information on policy compliance.

Although IFC, like OPIC, relies on client-reported data for some monitoring, unlike OPIC, IFC conducts site visits to all projects in its portfolio on a regular basis. IFC officials told us that using client-reported data for monitoring projects is a standard practice, but they underlined the difficulty in validating such data. According to IFC officials, its Environmental and Social team visits all projects once every 2 years. IFC also undertakes a limited number of post-completion evaluations to assess project impact. However, IFC employs a significantly larger staff than OPIC, including some in overseas field offices. For example, in 2012, IFC employed 3,763 people and managed a portfolio worth $45.8 billion, using about 17 times more human resources than OPIC to manage a portfolio that is about three times the size of OPIC's.

Conclusions

Given the difficult business climates in which many OPIC-supported projects operate, it is important that OPIC establish and follow robust selection and monitoring policies to ensure that it appropriately addresses project risks and can continue financing higher risk projects. OPIC has established policies and processes for reviewing, selecting, and monitoring projects, and in our review of a sample of projects we found that OPIC generally followed these policies. However, we found that in some cases project selection policies for human rights reviews needed to be accompanied by clearer guidance to ensure that decision makers had adequate information. With respect to its review of human rights issues, OPIC has recently issued guidance to clarify review responsibilities within OPIC, developed enhanced human rights due diligence processes, and hired additional specialized staff. In addition, OPIC has recently sought to enhance its process for assessing cumulative environmental and social impacts by adopting new guidelines that may support more systematic analyses.

Project monitoring is central to OPIC fulfilling its goals, particularly in difficult environments. OPIC's lack of requirements for timely documentation of site monitoring visits by OIP staff has resulted in site visit reports written several years after the visits occur. This can limit the usefulness of site visit findings for informing development impact projections and other decisions regarding ongoing and potential future projects. OPIC largely relies on client-reported data for annual updates for some projects, due in part to resource limitations that limit policy compliance site visits. This increases the potential that OPIC is relying on inaccurate or incomplete data. Thus, OPIC's current monitoring processes may not provide adequate information on projects' annual policy compliance and development impact status to support program goals.

Recommendations for Executive Action

To further improve OPIC's monitoring processes, we recommend that the President and CEO of OPIC take the following actions:

- Establish specific time frames, deadlines, or both for submission of site visit reports to OPIC's Executive Committee.

- Assess the current monitoring processes to ensure that the risk associated with the use of client-reported data and limited site visits for monitoring is acceptable for meeting OPIC's program goals.

AGENCY COMMENTS AND OUR EVALUATION

We provided a draft of this report to OPIC, State, Treasury, USTR, and USAID for comment. State, Treasury, USTR, and USAID did not provide any comments. In its written comments OPIC stated that it concurred with our two recommendations. With respect to our recommendation on ensuring timely completion of site visit reports, OPIC noted that its staff make presentations following site visits but that OPIC will incorporate our recommendation and the presentations into its monitoring policies. Regarding our recommendation on assessing its processes to ensure that current monitoring processes are acceptable for managing risks, OPIC stated that it has revised its development impact assessment process during the past year, and that it will use the input from this GAO audit in reviewing its monitoring process more generally over the coming year. In addition, OPIC provided technical comments on the draft report, and also provided us with additional information on how it conducts assessments of potential cumulative environmental and social impacts. Based on this information, we made revisions to the report as appropriate.

Kimberly M. Gianopoulos
Director, International Affairs and Trade

APPENDIX I: OBJECTIVES, SCOPE, AND METHODOLOGY

This report examines (1) the amounts and types of Overseas Private Investment Corporation's (OPIC) global financing support from fiscal year 2008 through fiscal year 2014, (2) how OPIC selects projects, and (3) how OPIC monitors projects.[70]

To analyze the amounts and types of OPIC's global financing support, we reviewed data provided by OPIC about its new commitments for fiscal years 2008 through 2014 to reflect recent activity. We used these data to characterize OPIC's new commitments for the period by financial instrument type, sector, and region, among other characteristics, for both the total value of and number of commitments. In addition to analyzing information about OPIC's overall new commitments for the period, we characterized and compared the projects committed during the fiscal year 2008 through 2014 period in four countries chosen for more in-depth analysis—Honduras, Kenya, Pakistan, and Peru. (For a description of our method for selecting these four countries, see below.) We also reviewed OPIC annual reports, developmental impact reports, and congressional budget justifications to obtain details about the agency's outstanding commitments, as well as information about its strategic priorities and actions during the period of analysis. To verify the accuracy of the OPIC- provided data and to better understand the classifications and sources used in its compilation we interviewed OPIC officials to discuss the collection and maintenance of these data. We also performed electronic data testing. Based on these activities, we determined that the data were reliable for our purpose of using them to analyze OPIC's new commitments for background and context, without impact on material findings in this report.

We also compiled data from World Bank sources to generate graphics and statements concerning OPIC commitment levels to countries based on the host countries' gross national per capita income and the ease of doing business ranking. We used the World Bank's per capita income data from the World Development Indicators database to categorize OPIC's commitments in fiscal years 2008 through 2014 to low, middle, or high income countries based on the World Bank's gross national income per capita for the project's host country in the year the OPIC commitment was made. To verify the reliability of these data, we reviewed publicly available documents regarding their collection, computation, and use. We determined the data were sufficiently reliable for the purpose described above.

We also used the World Bank's ease of doing business index rankings to determine the extent to which OPIC supported projects in countries with difficult business environments. This index is an annual ranking of the relative distance of countries from a best practices frontier score. The index is formed from observable components such as value added tax, gross domestic product deflators, and the number of procedures required to obtain permits or start a business. Because the index is a relative ranking, movements in the index must be interpreted in a relative context; we avoid interpretation errors by only using the index from a single year (2014). We also performed electronic data testing. We determined the data were sufficiently reliable for the purpose described above.

We selected a nongeneralizable sample of 21 projects that obtained OPIC financing support in four focus countries between fiscal years 2008 through 2014 to assess whether OPIC followed its policies and procedures for project selection and monitoring efforts. To select the four focus countries we limited ourselves to the 30 countries that are not members of the Organisation for Economic Co-operation and Development, whose total OPIC commitments were greater than $100 million. We further cut the list of countries to exclude two countries where either OPIC or the U.S. Agency for International Development (USAID) Inspector General had recently conducted audits. We cut an additional 14 countries from the list because they received a relatively small amount of OPIC funding or had a relatively high gross per capita income. Finally, we selected the four countries from the remaining list based on geographical dispersion, risk—including security risks, country governance and development indicators, and characteristics of the projects such as sector, development impact, and type of OPIC financial instrument. To select the 21 projects for our review, we considered several factors, including the project's (1) size relative to the total OPIC commitments in the country, (2) sector, (3) type of financing instrument, (4) age of the commitment, and (5) whether any disbursements had been made. In addition, in order to assure broad coverage of each country's committed projects, the team sought to achieve 40 percent coverage of both the number of projects in each selected country and the overall committed dollars.

To examine how OPIC selects projects for financing support, we met with officials from OPIC, Department of State (State), Department of the Treasury (Treasury), the Office of the U.S. Trade Representative (USTR), and USAID in Washington D.C.; the USAID Office of Inspector General, responsible for auditing OPIC; the former Director of OPIC's Office of Accountability; and nongovernmental organizations, including Friends of the Earth and the Accountability Counsel. In addition we obtained and reviewed OPIC policy documents, such as the finance policies and procedures and policies guiding the U.S. economic and host-country development impact, environmental and social, human rights, and worker rights clearances processes. We interviewed OPIC staff to discuss how they administer OPIC selection policies and procedures, including internal controls. We also interviewed State, Treasury, USTR, and USAID officials to discuss each agency's role on OPIC's Board of Directors, which is required to approve projects that exceed $50 million.

For our review of OPIC's project selection process, we developed a data collection instrument based on OPIC's project selection policies and conducted a review of the 21 projects based on OPIC-provided project documentation, such as project applications and policy clearance documents. Based on the questions in the data collection instrument we developed a method for analyzing the data against OPIC policies to develop our findings. Specifically, with the use of the data collection instrument, we reviewed how each project met eligibility requirements, including U.S. connections and additionality requirements; verified that OPIC finalized the four policy clearances for each project and reviewed the clearances for content; and reviewed applicable credit due diligence and character risk due diligence documentation. We did not review the sufficiency of OPIC's credit and legal due diligence processes while reviewing project documentation as this was outside the scope of our review.

We also visited two of the four focus countries, Honduras and Pakistan, to augment information we obtained from OPIC and other sources. In each country, we met with U.S. embassy and host-government officials, recipients of OPIC loans and loan guarantees, and officials from other development finance institutions. In addition, we visited some project sites.

To examine how OPIC monitors active projects' compliance with environmental and social, worker rights, and human rights policies and the U.S. economic and host-country development impact of these projects, we met with OPIC's Office of Investment Policy (OIP) to discuss its procedures for monitoring projects, collecting data, and validating data provided by its clients. As part of this review, we also discussed the procedures OPIC follows in case of missing or incomplete self-monitoring questionnaires (SMQs), which is the source for client-reported monitoring data. In addition, we met with OPIC officials to discuss OIP's monitoring site visit policies and methodology for selecting projects for site visits. We also examined the development impact profiles that OPIC develops prior to approving projects, which aim to assess each project's anticipated contribution to the development of the host country. We obtained OPICs development impact profile guidelines for scoring projects as developmental, highly developmental, or indeterminate. We interviewed the USAID Office of Inspector General and OPIC's Office of Accountability to discuss OPIC monitoring methodology and reports both offices had issued on specific audits of OPIC projects in

Turkey, Jordan, and Liberia. In addition we interviewed World Bank and International Finance Corporation officials about their monitoring procedures for similar activities, their indicators for assessing development outcomes, and the new harmonized indicators that several development finance institutions, including OPIC, are developing to standardize development impact information collection from clients.

We also developed a data collection instrument to review OPIC's compliance and impact monitoring efforts for the selected 21 projects. We focused on the following monitoring related issues:

- the presence of SMQs in project files, date of submission, and completeness of responses, including client responses regarding compliance with OPIC covenants and local laws and regulations;
- the presence of site visit reports and trip notes in project files, and the extent to which corrective actions or risks were identified during the course of site visits; and
- pre-selection development impact scores that project development impact outcomes for OPIC projects, and the re-scoring analyses conducted during a site visit, which measure the extent to which these projections have been achieved.

We used the data collection instrument to analyze changes in development impact scores for OPIC projects from initial to final estimates following site visits, if any, as well as to classify qualitative findings from OPIC clients' SMQs and site visit reports into broad categories. We did not review OPIC's processes for monitoring projects' financial performance.

The documentation we obtained for the 21 projects we reviewed supported our work for the second and third reporting objectives. These documents covered the topics and issues listed above, including OPIC's project selection and monitoring processes. To ensure completeness of our document files, we met with OPIC officials to discuss documentation for selected case study projects and changes to OPIC's requirements for project screening and monitoring documentation over time. When necessary we followed up with OPIC when the project files did not contain expected or required documents.

APPENDIX II: OVERSEAS PRIVATE INVESTMENT CORPORATION (OPIC) PROJECT COMMITMENTS IN SELECTED COUNTRIES FOR FISCAL YEARS 2008 THROUGH 2014

To provide detailed information on all OPIC projects for our selected focus countries, the tables below list the commitments OPIC made in fiscal years 2008 through 2014 in Honduras, Kenya, Pakistan, and Peru. For more information about our country selection methodology, see appendix I.

Table 5. Overseas Private Investment Corporation (OPIC) Commitments in Honduras for Fiscal Years 2008 through 2014

Fiscal year	U.S. entity	Project name/ foreign sponsor	Sector	Instrument	Project status as of 9/30/14[a]	Project description	Amount committed (dollars in millions)	Cumulative disbursed (dollars in millions)
2014	Citibank, N.A.	Grupo Jaremar	Manufacturing	Loan guarantee	Active	Proceeds of the loan will be used to fund new capital expenditure	20.57	20.57
2013	Citibank, N.A.	CGLOB-Banco Del Pais, S.A.	Financial services	Loan guarantee	Active	Expansion of small and medium enterprise lending portfolio	30.00	30.00
2012	Citibank, N.A.	Chous2-Banco Ficohsa	Financial services	Loan guarantee	Active	Expansion of small andmedium enterprise portfolio	22.50	22.50
2012	Wells Fargo, N.A.	W3-Banco Financiera Comercial Hondurena, S.A	Financial services	Loan guarantee	Active	Expansion of small and medium enterprise portfolio	15.00	15.00

Fiscal year	U.S. entity	Project name/ foreign sponsor	Sector	Instrument	Project status as of 9/30/14[a]	Project description	Amount committed (dollars in millions)	Cumulative disbursed (dollars in millions)
2010	Citibank, N.A.	Grupo Jaremar (Bufinsa, Indasa, Olepsa)	Manufacturing	Loan guarantee	Active	Diversified crude palm oil production and renewable energy	15.00	15.00
2009	Citibank, N.A.	CCA2-Digicel Honduras S.A. de CV	Communications	Loan guarantee	Not active	Cellular telecommunications network	15.00	15.00
2009	General Electric Company	Banco de America Central Honduras, S.A.(A)	Financial services	Loan guarantee	Active	Expansion of low-middle income mortgage lending	20.00	20.00
2009	General Electric Company	Banco de America Central Honduras, S.A.(B)	Financial services	Loan guarantee	Active	Expansion of small and medium enterprise lending portfolio	17.50	17.50
2008	Citibank, N.A.	CMFI-Org de Desarollo Empresarial Femen ODEF	Financial services	Loan guarantee	Not active	Microfinance institution	2.72	2.45
2008	Clark Realty Capital, LLC	Inter-Mac International, Inc.	Financial services	Direct loan	Active	Construction and sale/ lease of low income housing units	70.00	31.20
2008	Colite Outdoor, LCC	Colite Honduras, SA	Nonfinancial services	Political risk insurance	Not active	Billboards	2.88	0.00

Source: OPIC. | GAO-16-64

[a] "Active" refers to those commitments with either undisbursed commitments or active outstanding commitments, such as unrepaid loans and active insurance projects. "Not active" refers to those commitments that have either been cancelled or have no outstanding commitments, such as those commitments that have already been repaid.

Table 6. Overseas Private Investment Corporation (OPIC) Commitments in Kenya for Fiscal Years 2008 through 2014

Fiscal year	U.S. entity	Project name/ foreign sponsor	Sector	Instrument	Project status as of 9/30/14[a]	Project description	Amount committed (dollars in millions)	Cumulative disbursed (dollars in millions)
2014	Google Inc.	Lake Turkana Wind Power Limited	Manufacturing	Political risk insurance	Active	300 megawatt wind power project	46.00	0.00
2013	International School of Kenya Foundation	International School Of Kenya Limited	Nonfinancial services	Direct loan	Active	Campus expansion of the International School of Kenya	12.00	3.24
2013	New Globe School, Inc.	Bridge International Academies	Nonfinancial services	Direct loan	Active	Low-income private schools	10.00	4.00
2011	Access Africa Fund, LLC	Milango Financial Services Limited	Financial services	Political risk insurance	Not active	Loan	0.50	0.00
2011	David Gacheru	Eco-Metropolitan Development Co. Ltd.	Construction	Direct loan	Not active[b]	Housing construction	1.33	0.00
2011	Ormat International	Orpower 4 Geothermal	Energy -power generation	Loan guarantee	Active	Financing of geothermal power project	310.00	310.00
2009	Chemonics International	Not applicable	Nonfinancial services	Political risk insurance	Not active	Consulting services	0.18	0.00

Fiscal year	U.S. entity	Project name/ foreign sponsor	Sector	Instrument	Project status as of 9/30/14[a]	Project description	Amount committed (dollars in millions)	Cumulative disbursed (dollars in millions)
2009	Citibank, N.A.	CMFI-Kenya Women Finance Trust Ltd ("Kwft")	Financial services	Loan guarantee	Not active	Microfinance institution	4.56	4.10
2009	Citibank, N.A.	CMFI-Kenya Women Finance Trust Ltd. ("Kwft")	Financial services	Loan guarantee	Not active	Microfinance institution	2.67	2.40
2008	Citibank, N.A.	CMFI-Faulu Kenya	Financial services	Loan guarantee	Not active	Microfinance institution	4.56	4.10
2008	Citibank, N.A.	CMFI-K-Rep Bank	Financial services	Loan guarantee	Not active	Microfinance institution	7.22	6.50

Source: OPIC. | GAO-16-64

[a] "Active" refers to those commitments with either undisbursed commitments or active outstanding commitments, such as unrepaid loans and active insurance projects. "Not active" refers to those commitments that have either been cancelled or have no outstanding commitments, such as those commitments that have already been repaid.

[b] The project was later cancelled.

Table 7. Overseas Private Investment Corporation (OPIC) Commitments in Pakistan for Fiscal Years 2008 through 2014

Fiscal year	U.S. entity	Project name/ foreign sponsor	Sector	Instrument	Project status as of 9/30/14[a]	Project description	Amount committed (dollars in millions)	Cumulative disbursed (dollars in millions)
2014	Baigmohamed, Arif	Cinepax Corp.	Nonfinancial services	Direct loan	Active	Expansion of multiplex movie theater chain in various Pakistani cities	9.00	0.00
2014	General Electric Company	Master Wind Energy Limited	Energy - power generation	Loan guarantee	Active	50 megawatt wind power project in the Jhimpir wind corridor of southeastern Pakistan	50.00	0.00
2014	Hawa Holdings Limited	Hawa Energy	Energy -power generation	Loan guarantee	Active	50 megawatt wind power project in the Jhimpir wind corridor of southeastern Pakistan	97.70	0.00
2013	General Electric	Dewan Energy (PVT) Limited	Energy -power generation	Loan guarantee	Active	49.6 megawatt wind power project in the Jhimpir wind corridor of southeastern Pakistan	101.50	0.00
2013	General Electric	Sapphire Wind Power Company Limited	Energy -power generation	Loan guarantee	Active	Construction and operation of a 50 megawatt wind power plant	95.00	24.20

Fiscal year	U.S. entity	Project name/ foreign sponsor	Sector	Instrument	Project status as of 9/30/14[a]	Project description	Amount committed (dollars in millions)	Cumulative disbursed (dollars in millions)
2013	TPL Holdings Limited	TPL Trakker	Nonfinancial services	Direct loan	Active	Expansion of cargo security business	3.50	3.50
2012	Aga Khan Foundation USA	Aga Khan Hospital and Medical College Fund	Nonfinancial services	Direct loan	Active	Medical health care facility expansions in Pakistan	30.00	0.00
2012	Citibank, N.A.	Citibank N.A. Pakistan Branch	Financial services	Political risk insurance	Active	Branch banking services	150.00	0.00
2012	Citibank, N.A.	CGLOB-Pakistan Mobil Communication s Limited	Communications	Loan guarantee	Active	Expansion of mobile telecommunications infrastructure	33.33	28.95
2012	SSJD Energy	SSJD Bioenergy	Nonfinancial services	Direct loan	Active	Develop new 12 megawatt biomass power plant	16.70	0.00
2011	CHF International	Tameer Microfinance Bank Limited	Financial services	Loan guarantee	Not active[b]	Liquidity facility to support expansion of loan portfolio	21.50	0.00
2011	Mr. Muhammad Khan Chishti	TPL Properties (PVT) Limited	Construction	Direct loan	Active	Construction and medium term permanent loan for office building	20.00	20.00
2010	Chemonics International	Unknown	Nonfinancial services	Political risk insurance	Active	Consulting services	3.13	0.00
2010	Hyperbaric Technologies, Inc.	Not applicable	Nonfinancial services	Political risk insurance	Not active	Medical equipment	0.02	0.00
2010	Mustafa Koita	Towershare (PVT) Ltd.	Communications	Direct loan	Not active[b]	Construction of telecommunications towers	9.79	0.00

Table 7. (Continued)

Fiscal year	U.S. entity	Project name/ foreign sponsor	Sector	Instrument	Project status as of 9/30/14[a]	Project description	Amount committed (dollars in millions)	Cumulative disbursed (dollars in millions)
2008	CHF International	Tameer Microfinance Bank Limited	Financial services	Direct loan	Not active[b]	Microfinance lending and liquidity management	5.00	0.00
2008	Hyperbaric Technologies, Inc.	Directorate General Procurement	Nonfinancial services	Political risk insurance	Not active	Portable hyperbaric chambers	0.03	0.00

Source: OPIC. | GAO-16-64

[a] "Active" refers to those commitments with either undisbursed commitments or active outstanding commitments, such as unrepaid loans and active insurance projects. "Not active" refers to those commitments that have either been cancelled or have no outstanding commitments, such as those commitments that have already been repaid.

[b] The project was later cancelled.

Table 8. Overseas Private Investment Corporation (OPIC) Commitments in Peru for Fiscal Years 2008 through 2014

Fiscal year	U.S. entity	Project name/ foreign sponsor	Sector	Instrument	Project status as of 9/30/14[a]	Project description	Amount committed (dollars in millions)	Cumulative disbursed (dollars in millions)
2014	Antonio Galindez / Solarpack	Moquegua FV S.A.C.	Energy - power generation	Direct loan	Active	19 megawatt solar power plant in southern Peru to be built on a site adjacent to the Panamericana plant	41.50	6.80
2013	Citibank, N.A.	CMFI-2-Financiera Creditos Arequipos, S.A.	Financial services	Loan guarantee	Active	Microfinance institution	7.78	7.00
2013	Citibank, N.A.	CMFI-2-Financiera Edyficar, S.A.	Financial services	Loan guarantee	Active	Microfinance institution	7.78	7.00
2013	ContourGlobal	Humboldt Current (Peru)	Energy - power generation	Direct loan	Active	114 megawatt wind power generation project at two sites in northwestern Peru	192.76	0.00
2012	Accion International	MiBanco-IFC Syndication	Financial services	Direct loan	Active	Loan to support the portfolio expansion of MiBanco	20.00	20.00
2012	Conduit Capital Partners, LLC	Tacna Solar S.A.C. and Panamericana Solar	Energy - power generation	Loan guarantee	Active	Two 20 megawatt solar power plants	185.00	179.60

Table 8. (Continued)

Fiscal year	U.S. entity	Project name/ foreign sponsor	Sector	Instrument	Project status as of 9/30/14[a]	Project description	Amount committed (dollars in millions)	Cumulative disbursed (dollars in millions)
2012	Lucente Family Properties, LLC	Financiera TFC S.A.	Financial services	Political risk insurance	Not active	Consumer lending	0.50	0.00
2012	Lucente Family Properties, LLC	Total Artefactos S.A.	Nonfinancial services	Political risk insurance	Not active	Operation and expansion of retail stores	0.50	0.00
2011	Assured Guaranty	GTS Majes S.A.C. and GTS Reparticion S.A.C.	Energy - power generation	Loan guarantee	Active	Construction of solar power project	123.00	123.00
2011	GK Financing, LLC	Gamma Knife Peru	Nonfinancial services	Direct loan	Active	Installation/operation of stereotactic radiosurgery machine	2.06	2.06
2010	LFLP Holdings, LLC	Financiera TFC, S.A.	Financial services	Direct loan	Active	Expand portfolio of small and medium enterprise, micro-credit, and consumer loans	10.00	10.00
2010	Small Enterprise Assistance Funds	SEAF SME Debt Facility, LLC (Outsourcing Peru)	Transpor-tation	Direct loan	Not active	Provider of logistics support to importers and exporters	3.00	3.00
2010	Small Enterprise Assistance Funds	SEAF SME Debt Facility, LLC	Agriculture	Direct loan	Active	Exporter of mangos and tropical fruits	3.00	3.00

Fiscal year	U.S. entity	Project name/ foreign sponsor	Sector	Instrument	Project status as of 9/30/14[a]	Project description	Amount committed (dollars in millions)	Cumulative disbursed (dollars in millions)
		(Sunshine Export)						
2009	Chemonics International	Not applicable	Nonfinancial services	Political risk insurance	Not active	Consulting services	2.86	0.00
2009	GTV GloboKasNet LLC	GloboKas Peru S.A.C.	Manufacturing	Political risk insurance	Not active	Correspondent agent network	2.50	0.00
2009	Michael Deutschman and Gino Picasso	GloboKas Peru S.A.C.	Financial services	Direct loan	Active	Expansion of financial-telecom services business	2.50	2.50
2008	Wachovia Bank National Association	W-3 Banco Financiero Del Peru, S.A.	Financial services	Loan guarantee	Not active	Expansion of small and medium enterprise loan portfolio	10.00	10.00
2008	Wachovia Bank National Association	W-3 Banco Inter-americano de Finanzas, S.A.	Financial services	Loan guarantee	Not active	Expansion of residential mortgage portfolio	10.00	10.00

Source: OPIC. | GAO-16-64

[a] "Active" refers to those commitments with either undisbursed commitments or active outstanding commitments, such as unrepaid loans and active insurance projects. "Not active" refers to those commitments that have either been cancelled or have no outstanding commitments, such as those commitments that have already been repaid.

Appendix III: Descriptions of Select Overseas Private Investment Corporation (OPIC) Commitments in Four Countries, Fiscal Years 2008 through 2014

Below are summaries for 21 OPIC projects from 4 selected countries—Honduras, Kenya, Pakistan, and Peru—based on information we obtained from OPIC, as well as from our fieldwork.

Honduras

1. *Project:* CCA2 Digicel Honduras
   Purpose/Description: Loan guarantee through OPIC's Framework Guarantee Facility Agreement with Citibank to establish a cellular telecommunications network, with 990 cell tower sites and the capacity to service 1.4 million subscribers.
   Fiscal Year of Commitment: 2009
   Commitment Amount: $15 million
   Environmental Risk Category: B
   Expected Development Impact: Expand telecommunications infrastructure, create local jobs, and lower prices for cellular service, as well as support primary schools and mobile health clinics.
   U.S. Connection: Citibank N.A.
   Sector: Communications
   Status: Not active. The borrower paid off the loan in 2011.
2. *Project:* Banco del Pais
   Purpose/Description: Loan and loan guarantee through OPIC's Framework Guarantee Facility Agreement with Citibank to expand the facilities' small and medium sized enterprises lending portfolio, primarily in the areas of commercial, retail, real estate, services, and manufacturing.
   Fiscal Year of Commitment: 2013
   Commitment Amount: $30 million
   Environmental Risk Category: C
   Expected Development Impact: Support the provision of loans to small and medium sized enterprises for overlooked sectors and

support charitable activities in the host country including scholarships, clinics, orphanages, and schools.
U.S. Connection: Citibank N.A.
Sector: Financial services
Status: Active

3. *Project:* Inter-Mac International Inc.
   Purpose/Description: Support development of affordable housing and an affordable lease purchase payment program for low-income families.
   Fiscal Year of Commitment: 2008
   Commitment Amount: $70 million
   Environmental Risk Category: B
   Expected Development Impact: Provide affordable housing to an underserved portion of the Honduran population by encouraging the development of planned communities.
   U.S. Connection: Clark Enterprises, Inc. a U.S.-based realty company.
   Sector: Financial services
   Status: Active. As of April 2015, the project had built housing units inhabited by 500 residents, as well as schools and playgrounds. Delays in a planned government subsidy program have limited credit availability, slowing progress.
4. *Project:* Groupo Jaremar
   Purpose/Description: Loan guarantee through OPIC's South America Framework Facility Agreement with Citibank to refinance existing indebtedness and undertake capital expenditures related to expanding a palm oil plantation area, replacing boilers at two manufacturing facilities, and adding a bean processing production line along with other actions.
   Fiscal Year of Commitment: 2010
   Commitment Amount: $15 million
   Environmental Risk Category: B
   Expected Development Impact: Support the creation of local jobs with training and benefits, and the use of renewable fuels through the project company's production of biogas and biodiesel. In addition, generate foreign exchange earnings through exports to countries in Central and North America.
   U.S. Connection: Citibank N.A.
   Sector: Manufacturing
   Status: Active

5. *Project:* Groupo Jaremar
   Purpose/Description: Two loans under OPIC's Global Framework Guarantee Facility Agreement with Citibank to expand the company's existing operations in the country, including production of soap, oils, shortening, and margarine.
   Fiscal Year of Commitment: 2014
   Commitment Amount: $20.6 million
   Environmental Risk Category: B
   Expected Development Impact: Contribute to improved food security by increasing production and sale of a number of staple items.
   U.S. Connection: Citibank N.A.
   Sector: Manufacturing
   Status: Active

Kenya

6. *Project:* International School of Kenya Limited
   Purpose/Description: A campus expansion of the International School of Kenya, involving construction of a new elementary school, library, dining facility, faculty housing units, and infrastructure improvements.
   Fiscal Year of Commitment: 2013
   Commitment Amount: $12 million
   Environmental Risk Category: B
   Expected Development Impact: Support improvements in education infrastructure.
   U.S. Connection: U.S. directors and governors of The International School of Kenya Limited and the International School of Kenya Foundation.
   Sector: Nonfinancial services
   Status: Active
7. *Project:* Citibank Global Microfinance Framework Facility–K-Rep Bank
   Purpose/Description: Loan guarantee through OPIC's Global Framework Guarantee Facility Agreement with Citibank to raise the visibility of the microfinance sector among mainstream investors and

encourage the use of best practices and more sophisticated financing techniques in microfinance more widely.
Fiscal year of Commitment: 2008
Commitment Amount: $7.2 million
Environmental Risk Category: C
Expected Development Impact: Provide capital to microfinance institutions, benefitting income and quality of life for micro-entrepreneurs and their families.
U.S. Connection: Citibank N.A.
Sector: Financial services
Status: Not active

8. *Project:* Bridge International Academies Limited
Purpose/Description: A loan for the development and operation of 237 low-cost private schools, expanding facilities at 133 Bridge International Academies schools already operating in the country.
Fiscal Year of Commitment: 2013
Commitment Amount: $10 million
Environmental Risk Category: B
Expected Development Impact: Expand low cost preprimary and primary education, utilizing new technologies and management techniques.
U.S. Connection: New Globe School Inc.
Sector: Nonfinancial services
Status: Active

9. *Project:* Orpower 4 Geothermal
Purpose/Description: A loan to add up to 52 megawatts of additional generating capacity to an existing geothermal facility, through the installation of additional turbine units.
Fiscal Year of Commitment: 2011
Commitment Amount: $310 million
Environmental Risk Category: B
Expected Development Impact: Bring new capacity for supplying electricity through the national grid and provide newly hired staff with specialized training.
U.S. Connection: Ormat Technologies Inc.
Sector: Power generation
Status: Active

Pakistan

10. *Project:* Aga Khan Hospital and Medical College Foundation
    Purpose/Description: A loan to expand and renovate existing spaces at the Aga Khan medical health care facilities in Karachi by building an ambulatory care building, center for innovation in medical education, child care center, and a new private wing.
    Fiscal Year of Commitment: 2012
    Commitment Amount: $30 million
    Environmental Risk Category: B
    Expected Development Impact: Provide multiple health services under one roof, and bring free health care to poor patients by using the health service revenues from wealthier paying customers.
    U.S. Connection: Aga Khan Foundation U.S.A.
    Sector: Nonfinancial services
    Status: Active
11. *Project:* Dewan Energy Limited
    Purpose/Description: To operate a 50 megawatt wind power project in Pakistan's Jhimpir wind corridor.
    Fiscal Year of Commitment: 2013
    Commitment Amount: $101.5 million
    Environmental Risk Category: B
    Expected Development Impact: Help alleviate an acute shortage of electricity in Pakistan and increase the diversification of power away from high-priced imported fuel oil.
    U.S. Connection: General Electric International Inc.[71]
    Sector: Power generation
    Status: Active. The project was originally expected to be operational in 2015 but was delayed by a lengthy approval process with the government of Pakistan. The project's requests to extend the period for government approval of tariff conditions were denied by the government, as were subsequent appeals. According to OPIC, the project sponsor must evaluate whether it wishes to move ahead and whether it wishes to pursue further financing with OPIC; if so, OPIC would need to underwrite the project again.
12. *Project:* Pakistan Mobil Communications Ltd.
    Purpose/Description: Loan guarantee to Citibank under the Citibank Global Framework Agreement for its loan to Pakistan Mobil

Communications Ltd., to maintain and expand telecommunications coverage in Pakistan and install 3G equipment at existing cell towers.
Fiscal Year of Commitment: 2012
Commitment Amount: $33.3 million
Environmental Risk Category: B
Expected Development Impact: Support an expansion of telecommunications networks, with benefits including employment, training, local procurement and human capacity building.
U.S. Connection: Citibank N.A.
Sector: Communications Status: Active

13. *Project:* Tameer Microfinance Bank
Purpose/Description: Loan to reimburse Citibank supporting Tameer's loan portfolio growth plans and improving its asset liability. In addition, the loan is to extend Tameer's microfinance lending to support people affected by flooding in 2010.
Fiscal Year of Commitment: 2011
Commitment Amount: $21.5 million
Environmental Risk Category: C
Expected Development Impact: Support extension of microfinance loans to clients in the country, with a specific program for those affected by 2010 floods.
U.S. Connection: Cooperative Housing Foundation
Sector: Financial services
Status: Cancelled
14. *Project:* Sapphire Wind Power Company Ltd.
Purpose/Description: Loan guarantee to finance a 50 megawatt wind power project in Pakistan's Jhimpir wind corridor.
Commitment Fiscal Year: 2013
Commitment Amount: $95 million
Environmental Risk Category: B
Expected Development Impact: Expand renewable energy to the country's national grid, supporting the government's goal of diversifying power away from fuel oil, increase electricity supply, and bring advanced wind turbine equipment into the country.
U.S. Connection: General Electric Inc.[72]
Sector: Power generation
Status: Active
15. *Project:* TPL Properties, Ltd.

Purpose/Description: Loan to complete construction of an office tower building in Karachi.
Fiscal Year of Commitment: 2011
Commitment Amount: $20 million
Environmental Risk Category: B
Expected Development Impact: Introduce higher building standards and more sophisticated technology into Karachi's real estate market and attract national and international businesses as tenants.
U.S. Connection: A private U.S. citizen
Sector: Construction
Status: Active. According to OPIC, the borrower intends to prepay the loan and has applied for required approvals.

Peru

16. *Project:* Banco Financiero del Peru
Purpose/Description: Loan guarantee through OPIC's Global Framework Facilities Agreement with Wachovia Bank to expand small and medium enterprise lending throughout the country.
FY of Commitment: 2008
Commitment Amount: $10 million
Environmental Risk Category: C
Expected Development Impact: Expand lending to small and medium enterprises throughout the country.
U.S. Connection: Wachovia Bank
Sector: Financial services
Status: Not active
17. *Project:* Small Enterprise Assistance Fund SME Debt Facility LLC (Sunshine Exports)
Purpose/Description: Loan to help company finance working capital needs; complete the acquisition and lease repayment of recently added dehydration, freezing, and power equipment; and refinance the company's existing short-term debt.
Fiscal Year of Commitment: 2010
Commitment Amount: $3 million
Environmental Risk Category: B
Expected Development Impact: Provide employment opportunities in rural, high poverty areas in the north of the country and introduce new

production technologies to the local industry that will increase product lines and increase foreign exchange earnings through exports.

U.S. Connection: Small Enterprise Assistance Fund

Sector: Agriculture

Status: Active

18. *Project:* Small Enterprise Assistance Fund SME Debt Facility LLC (Outsourcing Peru S.A.C.)

    Purpose/Description: Loan to purchase the land and support the reconfiguration of space in an existing warehouse in Lima, including purchase of new racks, roofs, and office equipment. Proceeds will also be used to purchase a small fleet of trucks and special trailers to handle increased business volume.

    Fiscal year of Commitment: 2010

    Commitment Amount: $3 million

    Environment Risk Category: B

    Expected Development Impact: Provide warehouse and storage facilities for processing, distribution, and logistics services for freight and cargo.

    U.S. Connection: Small Enterprise Assistance Fund

    Sector: Transportation

    Status: Not active

19. *Project:* Tacna Solar S.A.C. and Panamericana Solar S.A.C.

    Purpose/Description: Loan guarantee to support Conduit Capital Partners' investment to build two solar electricity generation plants in Peru. Electricity generated to be sold to Peru's national grid and support diversification of electrical generation in a poor rural area of Peru.

    Fiscal Year of Commitment: 2012

    Commitment Amount: $185 million

    Environmental Risk Category: B

    Expected Development Impact: Improve local capacity by providing worker training and by expanding logistics services for local companies.

    U.S. Connection: Conduit Capital Partners LLC

    Sector: Power generation

    Status: Active

20. *Project:* GTS Majes S.A.C. and GTS Reparticion S.A.C.

Purpose/Description: Loan guarantee to support the development, construction and operation of two 20-megawatt solar power projects in the country.
Fiscal Year of Commitment: 2011
Commitment Amount: $123 million
Environmental Risk Category: B
Expected Development Impact: Expand capacity of the national grid through the generation of two new solar electric plants. In addition, expand employment and human capacity through the installation of advanced solar panel equipment in rural areas.
U.S. Connection: Assured Guaranty Municipal Corp.
Sector: Power generation
Status: Active

21. *Project:* Gamma Knife Peru
Purpose/Description: Operation of a Gamma Knife center at the Peruvian Air Force Hospital in Lima that will provide detection and treatment of tumors in military personnel and the general public.
Commitment date: 2011
Commitment Amount: $2.1 million
Environmental Risk Category: B
Expected Development Impact: Transfer technology by utilizing new medical technologies and offering new services in the host country, and promote private sector development through local procurement.
U.S. Connection: GK Financing LLC
Sector: Nonfinancial services
Status: Active

APPENDIX IV: OVERSEAS PRIVATE INVESTMENT CORPORATION (OPIC) DEVELOPMENT IMPACT SCORING

OPIC officials score projects using applicant-provided data, which include both quantitative information (e.g., expected number of jobs) and qualitative information (e.g., new technique introduced). OPIC currently characterizes projects' development impact as indeterminate (1-24), developmental (25-59), and highly developmental (60-100). Table 9 illustrates the development impact scoring for a wind power project in Pakistan that was scored as highly developmental.

Table 9. Example of the Overseas Private Investment Corporation's (OPIC) Development Impact Indicators and Scoring for a Wind Power Project in Pakistan

Development indicator	Sub-indicator	Maximum score	Project score
Jobs and human capacity building		**25**	**10**
	Job creation	15	5
	Training	5	5
	Employment benefits	5	0
Demonstration effects		**20**	**10**
	New product/ technique	10	2.5
	Sector Impact	5	5
	Local ownership stake	5	2.5
Host-country impact		**20**	**7.5**
	Local procurement	15	5
	Fiscal impact	2.5	2.5
	Foreign exchange impact	2.5	0
Environmental and community benefits		**15**[a]	**15**
	Community benefit	10	10
	Environmental benefits	10	10
Development reach		**20**	**20**
Total development impact score		**100**	**62.5**

Source: OPIC. | GAO-16-64

[a] According to OPIC's policy, although the social benefits and environmental benefits sub-indicators may have a maximum score of 10 point each, the combined point total for this indicator is 15 points.

End Notes

[1] Commitment occurs when OPIC creates the budgetary or financial obligation for a project.

[2] The World Bank's ease of doing business index ranks countries according to a variety of factors that affect the business climate. For this analysis, we divided the 189 countries in the index into quartiles according to their 2014 ranking. Quartile 1, Quartile 2, and Quartile 3 each include 47 countries, and Quartile 4 includes 48 countries.

[3] Congress established OPIC in 1969 through the Foreign Assistance Act of 1961. Pub .L. No. 87-195, Pt. I, § 231, as added by Pub. L. No. 91-175, Pt. I, § 105 et seq., Dec. 30, 1969.

[4] Under the Federal Credit Reform Act of 1990, agencies, including OPIC, are required to estimate and request appropriations for the long-term costs, or subsidy costs, of their credit activities (Pub. L. No. 101-508, Title XIII, § 13201 (Nov. 5, 1990), codified at 2 U.S.C. §§ 661-661f). According to OPIC, the subsidy cost estimates take into account, among other things, interest and fees it charges its customers for loans, loan guarantees, and insurance, as well as estimated default costs.

[5] According to OPIC, because the U.S. government is liable for the risks, Congress limits OPIC's total liability annually.

[6] 22 U.S.C. § 2195(a).

[7] The position of Director of the Office of Accountability has been vacant since October 2014.

[8] According to OPIC, commitments do not correspond directly to the number of projects. When OPIC provides two different products for the same project, such as a direct loan and political risk insurance, it reports two distinct financial commitments but only counts the project once.

[9] According to OPIC data, 6 out of 718 of OPIC's new commitments in fiscal years 2008 through 2014 were for amounts larger than $250 million, and 5 of these were loan guarantees.

[10] The New independent states category comprises countries in the former Soviet Union.

[11] OPIC committed over $950 million to cross-regional projects from fiscal year 2008 through 2014.

[12] 22 U.S.C. § 2191(2).

[13] Following OPIC's methodology, we used the U.S. gross national product implicit price deflator to calculate low, middle, and high per capita income thresholds for each fiscal year from 2008 through 2014.

[14] A 1978 House Conference Report noted that "It is understood, however, that there will be certain categories of exceptions which may be approved by the OPIC Board of Directors or certain individual exceptions, such as projects with a unique developmental impact, determined on a case-by-case basis by the OPIC Board. Among OPIC's present categories of exceptions are small business and cooperative projects and mineral and energy projects." See H.R. Conf. Rep. 95-1043, 95th Cong., Apr. 5, 1978.

[15] We categorized OPIC's commitments in fiscal years 2008 through 2014 by country and value using the World Bank gross national income per capita for the relevant countries.

[16] Power generation projects include electricity generation (including renewable energy projects), electricity distribution services, energy efficiency projects, electric services, and rural electrification projects, among other categories.

[17] Nonfinancial services projects include those that provide medical, humanitarian, education, and consulting services, among other services.

[18] See app. I for more information about our country selection methodology.

[19] OPIC has agreements, called framework agreements, with large financial institutions for which OPIC agrees to guarantee a certain percentage, typically 75 percent, of the value of each loan approved under the agreement. The framework partner is responsible for conducting all credit underwriting and due diligence responsibilities of the potential loans made by the framework partner under the agreement.

[20] OPIC also conducts initial background checks, credit checks, or both during the screening step. We did not review OPIC's processes for conducting these checks.

[21] OPIC was unable to provide us with the number of commitments it has made to nonprofits organized in the U.S. with foreign governing boards.

[22] See app. I for information concerning our methodology for selecting the 21 projects for review. For this review of project documentation, we verified that OPIC made specific decisions or judgments per OPIC policies and congressionally mandated requirements, approved various decisions, and documented the process. We did not review each decision or judgment against OPIC policies to verify its accuracy.

[23] The statute also does not allow OPIC to provide direct loans for a project involving the extraction of oil or gas. In addition, OPIC must limit direct loans for projects involving mining or extraction of non-fuel ores or minerals to $4 million per year. 22 U.S.C. § 2194(c).

[24] With regard to OPIC, Congress defined a small business as a company which is below the Fortune 1000 (H.R. Conf. Rep. 95-1043, Apr. 5, 1978). According to OPIC officials, they use figures significantly below the Fortune 1000 threshold to define small businesses.

[25] According to OPIC officials, prior to 2012, OPIC determined project additionality on the basis of country-wide assessments of risk that would affect private sector investment, as well as project-specific factors. In consultation with its congressional authorizing committee in 2012, OPIC changed its approach to assessing additionality. According to OPIC policy, OPIC now asks all applicants to certify whether they have evaluated the availability of private sector financing. For projects in countries with high country risk ratings, OPIC can still provide financing if applicants answer no to that question.

[26] Staff are to review business plans, financial statements, draft contracts, and other documents in accordance with OPIC policy. OPIC staff are also to obtain independent information on the country, market, and other project aspects. Staff are also to request information from the U.S. Embassy in the project country relating to potential ties to terrorism, money laundering, corruption, or other violations of local law.

[27] According to OPIC policy, character risk due diligence includes the investigation of an applicant's possible involvement in terrorism, corrupt practices, money laundering, and other criminal activities. Officials are also required to review the project company's Anti-Money Laundering and Know Your Customer policies, internal controls, and past actions with regard to social responsibility, corporate image, and environmental accountability.

[28] We did not independently review OPIC's credit and character risk due diligence reviews. However, clients we interviewed cited instances of OPIC's reviews identifying concerns that resulted in significant project modifications. For example, OPIC identified a project contractor with a copyright infringement issue that led the client to terminate that contract, and it also determined that one of the client's contracts was inappropriately priced, enabling the client to reduce the cost of the contract by $5 million.

[29] The character risk due diligence issue concerned a foreign supplier for a renewable energy project in Pakistan. OPIC decided to proceed with the project because the foreign supplier did not appear on any U.S. sanctions lists and a U.S. company working with the foreign supplier performed its own due diligence and stated that it was not violating any U.S. sanctions laws by contracting with the supplier. OPIC also developed a work plan for areas of continued due diligence, including the review of the project investor's anti-money laundering policies and practices.

[30] OPIC officials use the policies in effect on the date of the client's application when conducting policy clearances.

[31] 22 U.S.C. § 2191(i), § 2191(k)(1).

[32] 22 U.S.C. § 2199(h), § 2200a(1).

[33] OPIC, *Annual Report on Development Impact: Fiscal Year 2013* (Washington, D.C.: Sept. 2014).

[34] 22 U.S.C. § 2191b.

[35] Projects whose applications were signed before October 15, 2010, are subject to the *OPIC Environmental Handbook* published in 2004.

[36] IFC is a member of the World Bank Group and is the largest global development finance institution. It works with the private sector in developing countries. According to OPIC officials, IFC's Performance Standards are viewed as best practices by development finance institutions. IFC updated the performance standards in 2012.

[37] Prior to OPIC's enactment of the Environmental and Social Policy Statement in 2010, OPIC categorized projects as A, B, C, D, E, or F projects.

[38] Category A projects are those projects with the most potential to have significant, adverse environmental or social impacts that are irreversible, sensitive, diverse, or unprecedented. Examples may include large-scale industrial plants and power transmission projects, pipelines for large-scale transport of oil, and all projects with potentially major impacts on indigenous peoples.

[39] OPIC's Board of Directors is prohibited by law from voting in favor of any OPIC action that is likely to have significant adverse environmental impacts that are sensitive, diverse, or unprecedented unless an environmental impact assessment or audit has been made available to the U.S. public, locally affected groups in the host country, and host-country nongovernmental organizations for at least 60 days. 22 U.S.C. § 2191a(b).

[40] The categorical prohibitions also include those projects in or impacting natural World Heritage Sites, or in or impacting United Nations National Parks or Protected Areas; construction of dams that significantly and irreversibly disrupt natural ecosystems, alter natural hydrology, inundate large land areas, impact biodiversity, displace large numbers of inhabitants, or impact local inhabitants' ability to earn a livelihood; require resettlement of more than 5,000 people; and production or trade in radioactive materials.

[41] Federal law requires that OPIC only support a project if the host country is taking steps to adopt and implement laws that extend internationally recognized worker rights. The law further requires OPIC to include a clause in OPIC agreements stating that investors agree (1) not to prevent employees from freely associating or collectively bargaining, and (2) to observe applicable laws relating to child labor, minimum wages, hours of work and occupational and health and safety, and not to use forced labor. 22 U.S.C. § 2191a(a)(1).

[42] The Generalized System of Preferences program is administered by USTR and provides preferential duty-free treatment for over 3,500 products from a wide range of designated beneficiary countries.

[43] See 19 U.S.C. § 2462. These rights include the right of association and a prohibition on the use of any form of forced or compulsory labor.

[44] OPIC's policy statement states that projects in locations, industries, and sectors with a clear history of labor rights issues are higher risk. Such projects may involve significant construction, manual harvesting of agricultural commodities, or extractive industries, which may present circumstances that make it difficult for workers to exercise trade union rights and/or have a higher likelihood that forced or child labor is employed. Prior to 2010, OPIC did not have a Special Considerations category for projects based on worker rights issues.

[45] 22 U.S.C. § 2191(i).

[46] State must review (1) all potential OPIC projects in countries that are deemed "most sensitive," (2) all projects in countries deemed "sensitive" that also are either related to security services or for which the host government has more than 50 percent involvement. OPIC conducts the human rights clearances for those projects in countries deemed "less sensitive" and those deemed "sensitive" that are not in a sensitive sector. OPIC also agreed to provide State with a summary list of all human rights clearances issued by both OPIC and State on the first of each month.

[47] According to OIP officials, the clearance process does not encompass a review of all the human rights contained in the Universal Declaration for Human Rights, and it only reviews those human rights that private companies can impact.

[48] We did not determine whether this OPIC documentation covered all potentially relevant human rights issues.

[49] Projects less than or equal to $20 million require credit approval from the Managing Director of Credit Policy and management approval from the Vice President of the originating department. Projects between $20 million and $50 million require credit approval from the Credit Committee and management approval from the Investment Committee. Projects greater than $50 require credit approval from the Credit Committee and management approval from the Investment Committee and Board of Directors.

[50] According to OPIC, the Board of Directors retains the right to require any projects to be brought to it for review and approval for any reason it chooses. For example, all investment funds and any commitment that will cause OPIC's aggregate exposure to a customer to exceed $50 million require board approval. In addition, the board has, at times, required that commitments for projects in certain sectors, such as housing, be brought to the board regardless of the commitment amount.

[51] Office of Accountability. *OA Review: Buchanan Renewable Energy Projects in Liberia* (Washington, D.C.: September 2014).

[52] The Joint Explanatory Statement accompanying the Consolidated and Further Continuing Appropriations Act, 2015, required OPIC to submit within 90 days to the committees on appropriations OPIC's management plan for implementing the Office of Accountability's 2014 recommendations pertaining to Liberia (160 Cong. Rec. H9954, 2014).

[53] According to OPIC, the draft changes to the policy statement will be submitted for public comment when the revisions are complete. OPIC expects to publish the updated Environmental and Social Policy Statement for public comment in early 2016.Officials told us that they initially planned to finalize the policy statement and manual by April 1, 2016 but that they will not meet the planned date.

[54] Two of the four wind power projects discussed in this section were included in the sample of 21 projects that we reviewed. We identified the other two wind power projects from a list of new commitments that OPIC made between fiscal years 2008 and 2014.

[55] The OPIC-contracted cumulative impact assessment completed in October 2015 found that the government of Pakistan has approved 25 wind power projects in this region as of 2015.

[56] The OPIC-contracted cumulative impact assessment was completed in October 2015 and OPIC received the final report in November 2015.

[57] Under certain atmospheric and lighting conditions, rotating wind turbine blades can create a rapidly alternating series of light and shadow known as shadow flicker which, under particular and very infrequent conditions, can induce seizures in people with photosensitive epilepsy and is documented to be a nuisance for some people.

[58] With the inclusion of these conditions, OPIC can require the project companies to adjust their activities to be in accordance with policy—such as noise level guidelines.

[59] The Department of Financial and Portfolio Management's monitoring efforts focus on financial performance, compliance with financial covenants, and repayment status through analysis of financial statements, rating agency reports, financial models, and engineering reports. The Investment Funds Department's monitoring efforts focus on the financial performance of the companies within each investment fund's portfolio, the fund managers' value addition during the holding period, and the successful execution of an exit strategy for each investment.

[60] OPIC did not provide an example of when a missing SMQ triggered a site visit. For the 1 project in our sample of 21 projects that did not turn in SMQs for several years, OIP did not conduct a site visit.

[61] The site visit data do not include those site visits conducted by other groups within OPIC. According to OPIC, the Department of Financial and Portfolio Management and the Legal Affairs Department conducted a combined average of 106 monitoring site visits per year during the fiscal year 2009 through 2014 period. This monitoring is coordinated with OIP to maximize OPIC's total project oversight. These site visits provide key financial monitoring

information and an information stream for OIP. For example, OIP may use information gathered from other departments' monitoring efforts to inform and prioritize its own monitoring activities.

[62] According to OPIC officials, the form expired and the SMQ has been redesigned to more closely parallel the data gathered during the project application process. Going forward, officials said, they will use the new form during their site visits.

[63] According to OPIC officials, several of the projects in our sample are either not yet operational or had not been operational long enough to justify a monitoring site visit.

[64] The focus of the 2-day visit was to review documentation as well as practices and procedures for monitoring air emissions, wastewater, solid waste, and hazardous materials handling. The Environmental and Social Group concluded that the client company had good documentation regarding the environmental measuring and monitoring processes and procedures.

[65] Each group within OIP conducts distinct site visits to monitor issues in its field of specialization; however, to reduce logistical burdens, they may coordinate site monitoring when possible.

[66] GAO, *Standards for Internal Control in the Federal Government*, GAO/AIMD-00-21.3.1 (Washington, D.C.: November 1999).

[67] OPIC is statutorily required to monitor the economic and social development impact and benefits of its projects and report this information to Congress annually. 22 U.S.C. § 2199(g)-(h); 22 U.S.C. § 2200a(a)(1).

[68] GAO/AIMD-00-21.3.1.

[69] Office of Accountability. *OA Review: Buchanan Renewable Energy Projects in Liberia* (Washington, D.C.: September 2014).

[70] We limited the time frame to the fiscal year 2008 through 2014 period for all three objectives to ensure a consistent comparison of OPIC's recent activities as well as (1) to include any recent shifts in commitments or selection and monitoring processes that might have arisen due to shifts in OPIC priorities, policies, or procedures; (2) to ensure that projects selected for a more in-depth review of OPIC's selection and monitoring processes included projects that had reached operational status and had been monitored by OPIC; and (3) to limit the number of projects operating under different policies due to the evolution of OPIC's selection policies.

[71] General Electric is to provide operations and maintenance services to the project for 10 years, services worth at least 25 percent of project costs.

[72] General Electric is expected to supply wind turbine generators and provide operations and maintenance support through a subcontract to a Chinese company.

INDEX

P

Q

R

S

T

U

V

W